Endeavor®

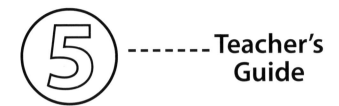
5 -------Teacher's Guide

New Readers Press®
ProLiteracy's publishing division

Endeavor® 5: Teacher's Guide
ISBN 978-1-56420-873-6

Copyright © 2009 New Readers Press
New Readers Press
ProLiteracy's Publishing Division
104 Marcellus Street, Syracuse, New York 13204
www.newreaderspress.com

Printed in the United States of America

18

Proceeds from the sale of New Readers Press materials support professional development, training, and technical assistance programs of ProLiteracy that benefit local literacy programs in the U.S. and around the globe.

Contributing Author: Vista Resources, Inc.
Developmental Editors: Ellen Northcutt, Donna Townsend
Creative Director: Andrey Woodbury
Production Specialist: Maryellen Casey

Contents

Strategies for Success with *Endeavor*

Tips for Planning Instruction

There are a number of strategies that you can implement to maximize the effectiveness of *Endeavor's* lesson plans. First, always prepare your lessons before class. This includes reading and practicing the text of the story, selecting activities, and preparing materials. Although the *Endeavor* Teacher's Guide is intended to provide ideas and guidance, it is not meant as a script. Use the explanations in the Teacher's Guide to help you develop explanations in your own words. Additionally, modify the questions, examples, and activities to suit the needs of your students. If, for example, some students need more time to complete an element in the lesson, determine which activities you can omit or shortcut in order for students to have the time they need to be successful. Remember, the objective is for students to feel satisfaction as they become aware of their gains in building reading, writing, and other language skills.

Tips for Implementing Instruction

Students should be clear about what is expected of them. Therefore, inform students of the learning goals and outcomes before beginning a lesson. This Teacher's Guide provides learning objectives on the first page of notes for each lesson. Students should also be clear about how they will perform the tasks required of them. It is imperative, therefore, that you model every new skill, and model skills again if your students have not practiced them in a while. For example, model a sentence that uses a new vocabulary word correctly and in a meaningful context, and then work with students to explain what made your sentence effective. This kind of explicit skill modeling will make your expectations clear to your students. Students will begin to internalize what constitutes a complete answer or a meaningful interaction with a text.

In addition to modeling skills, you will also want to model strategies. Create your own Think About Its to complement those incorporated in the student book. Modeling how you think as you read will provide students with concrete examples of the ways that they should be interacting with text. If you realize that your students have never taken notes as they read, model notetaking. Use a text photocopied onto an overhead transparency and demonstrate how you highlight relevant passages or take notes on the side of the text. The more specific you are and the more examples you give of the various skills and strategies, the clearer the understanding will be in students' minds. Use of the active reading strategies should become second nature to students. This will occur with repetition, so remind them to use strategies that they have already learned.

Fluency and vocabulary development are important components of your students' reading growth. Therefore, you and your students should read aloud whenever possible. Not only will students get to listen to your fluent model and practice their own oral fluency, but students' reading will provide an opportunity for you to do informal assessments. Similarly, the Vocabulary Knowledge Rating Chart (Master 9) can help you to assess your students' facility with words and can inform your vocabulary instruction. If, for instance, most of your students indicate that they fully understand the word *bruised*, but the word *permeated* is unfamiliar, spend your instructional time on the unfamiliar word. Additionally, spend more time on the words that students are likely to encounter in a variety of texts—the key vocabulary words—rather than specialized vocabulary. There are activities and suggestions throughout the Teacher's Guide to assist you in your explanations and planning.

Tips for Maximizing Students as Resources

The life experience of adult learners is invaluable, so make sure that you are bringing students' prior knowledge into every aspect of your teaching. Make your examples relevant to students' experience, and allow them to draw connections between what they are learning and what they already know. The stories and articles in *Endeavor* were selected because they are likely in some way to relate to students' life experiences and concerns. Find those connections, and make them clear to students.

In addition to utilizing students' prior knowledge in your lessons, use students as resources for themselves and one another. The Revising and Editing Checklist (Master 11) is provided as a tool for students. They can check and improve their own and their peers' work using very specific criteria. As always, model the use of the Revising and Editing Checklist, and give students ample opportunity to practice with it. Also, have students use the Writing Rubric (Master 10) to evaluate their completed pieces against measures of ideas, organization, voice, and conventions. Compare your evaluations with theirs as part of writing conferences. These strategies for self- and peer-evaluation do not preclude the need for teacher assessment, but they do give students another set of eyes as they review their own work. The Revising and Editing Checklist and the Writing Rubric allow students to work with and eventually internalize criteria for an acceptable piece of writing.

Assessment is the key to determining if your instruction has been successful and if your students are progressing. You should be using periodic formal assessments, such as the TABE (Tests of Adult Basic Education) or another instrument, to track your students' progress. Informal assessments are important as well, particularly when it comes to modifying your instruction from lesson to lesson. Informal assessments include checklists of skills, over-the-shoulder analyses of students' reading, and your evaluations of students' class work. Although *Endeavor* provides rich resources in terms of texts, activities, strategies, and pedagogy, ultimately it is you, the teacher, who is most important to your students' success. It is your preparation, modeling, and evaluation that will ensure that your students are growing as learners, readers, and writers. We welcome you and wish you luck as you embark on this *Endeavor*.

Suggestions for Developing Vocabulary

Key Vocabulary

The key vocabulary words have been chosen because they are likely to be entirely unfamiliar or somewhat unfamiliar to many students. By working with these words before students begin reading, you are giving students additional keys with which to unlock the meaning of the text. The more they know before reading, the more they are likely to take with them from the reading.

In addition to helping students comprehend a particular text, vocabulary study will provide students with new words to add to their working vocabularies. As their vocabularies grow, they will be able to read increasingly more complex texts. They will also be able to express themselves in a more sophisticated manner in their writing and speaking.

Side-Column Vocabulary

Vocabulary words can be broken down into three tiers. Tier 1 words are the most basic words. These words (like *shoe*, *paper*, and *sad*) do not need to be taught, because they are already part of students' vocabularies. Tier 2 words (like *exertion*, *unanimous*, and *rickety*) are found in more sophisticated texts and across a variety of domains. These are the kinds of words that have been selected as key vocabulary words.

Tier 3 words (like *creditor*, *pedometer*, and *prosecution*) are specialized vocabulary. These words appear infrequently in texts and generally apply only to specific domains. These are the kinds of words that have been selected as side-column vocabulary. Although it will be useful to teach these words in the context of the particular text you are reading, they are not likely to appear frequently or in a variety of texts. Therefore, *Endeavor* focuses more on direct instruction and practice of Tier 2 words than it does on Tier 3 words.

How to Use the Vocabulary Knowledge Rating Chart

The Vocabulary Knowledge Rating Chart (Master 9) is a quick tool for determining students' prior knowledge of each of the vocabulary words. Not only will it help students focus on each of the words, but it will give you a sense of the words on which you will want to concentrate instruction.

Model the use of the Vocabulary Knowledge Rating Chart when you first introduce it. Once students are familiar with the chart, however, they should be able to use it on subsequent sets of words quickly and without extensive instruction.

Tips for Teaching Vocabulary

- The key to learning vocabulary is practice. Each lesson guide includes a number of different strategies for vocabulary practice. Provide as many opportunities as possible for students to interact with and practice the new words.

- Be sure to reframe students' sentences if they are using words incorrectly, and provide additional examples and explanations if necessary. If students learn vocabulary words incorrectly, they will use them incorrectly in the future.

- Use challenging vocabulary when you are talking to your students. Your modeling will help them use words in appropriate contexts, and the unfamiliar words you use will encourage students to explore vocabulary beyond what is being explicitly taught.

- Encourage students to use their new vocabulary words in their everyday lives, and invite them to share anecdotes of when they use the words or encounter the words in conversations or in the media.

Suggestions for Keeping Personal Dictionaries

Personal dictionaries are meant both as spelling aids and as places to record and explore new vocabulary words. For maximum benefit, personal dictionaries should be user-friendly.

A personal dictionary can be created from a notebook or from paper stapled or bound together. It should be its own entity rather than part of another notebook. This will make it more easily accessible and portable as students move through various levels of *Endeavor*. The personal dictionary should be organized alphabetically and have at least four full pages for each letter, perhaps fewer for the less frequently used letters.

Since vocabulary words are best internalized when they are used often, it is important that personal dictionaries be interactive. Students should enter new words they encounter from their experience and from the texts and other print material they are reading. Ask them to include a clear definition and part of speech along with sentences, examples, sketches, or other means for them to internalize a full, clear meaning of the term. Students should have a voice in deciding what to include in an entry.

Plan frequent activities that require students to return to the words they have recorded. Have students find a "k" word and share it with a neighbor; dramatize a "p" word and have the class guess it; sketch a simple drawing of a word; or write a sentence, correctly using at least three of their vocabulary words. If students simply enter the words and never return to them, the benefit of the personal dictionary will be minimal.

Inside the front and back covers of the personal dictionary, have students record words that are particularly challenging for them to spell. This will limit the number of times they need to search for those words in a large dictionary. It also gives the teacher a place to record words that students are consistently misspelling in their writing. Finally, it ensures that the personal dictionary is being utilized often, as it will be on students' desks as they are writing.

Suggestions for Writing Portfolios

A writing portfolio is intended to hold student work so that the student, teacher, or observer can see how the student has developed as a writer. A portfolio can be a file folder, a box, or a large envelope. Ask each student to create his or her own portfolio. Portfolios can include any writing that the student has done. If the class is producing a lot of work, you will want to pick and choose items for the portfolio so that it doesn't become unmanageable and unusable. Encourage students to include pieces that they are particularly proud of. The goal is to have the contents organized and accessible.

By reviewing their portfolios, students, and particularly adult students, will have the opportunity to evaluate their own work and growth. They will also have access to the teacher's observations and evaluations of their work. Moreover, portfolios might include copies of the Writing Rubric (Master 10) which students can use to evaluate and comment on their own work. Self-evaluations of final drafts of writing can be modeled by the teacher and done often.

Writing portfolios should be interactive rather than stored out of reach. Students use them to review their work and note their progress. In addition, students should have the opportunity to return to a piece they have written, work to improve it, and then publish it in a creative way. By continuing to interact with their writing and evaluating their own progress, students will remain motivated to improve their writing.

Developing Fluency

Fluency is a reader's ability to recognize words automatically and accurately and to read aloud with appropriate expression. The expression is called *prosody*, and it includes intonation, stress, rate, rhythm, and phrasing. Prosody is important to a reader's understanding of the text. Students must comprehend what they are reading in addition to reading quickly and accurately; therefore, teachers must effectively model and teach prosody. And students need repetition in order to develop fluency.

Although the teacher is an important model of fluent reading, the teacher cannot work individually with every student at the same time. Also, in any group of readers, there are likely to be some differences in students' ability to read orally. Therefore, strategies have been developed to help classrooms of readers at different levels to work on fluency simultaneously. These strategies usually include modeling and repetition.

Fluency in *Endeavor*

Endeavor supports you as you work with your students to improve their fluency. Each lesson in the Teacher's Guide provides strategies you can use to practice fluency. With any of the texts, you may wish to use other strategies in addition to those described in the lesson.

Strategies

Echo Reading—With Echo Reading, students imitate fluent reading modeled by the teacher. The teacher reads aloud, and the students are the echo. Depending upon the level of the readers in your class, you will break the

text into phrases or full sentences. Read the phrase or sentence aloud, paying careful attention to your accuracy and prosody. Then have the class repeat the phrase or sentence, also paying careful attention to accuracy and prosody. Continue reading aloud and having the class echo you for the rest of the passage. Be sure to break the text at logical points in order to maintain the meaning of the text.

Choral Reading—Choral Reading involves students reading aloud together, like a chorus. The teacher begins by reading the chosen passage aloud, concentrating on accuracy and prosody. Then students read the same passage aloud in groups ranging from three students to the whole class reading together. In order to set and maintain the pace, the teacher reads aloud with the students. Choral Reading allows readers the opportunity to practice fluency in a situation where they are supported by other readers.

Paired Repeated Reading—Paired Repeated Reading involves students working with one another—rather than one-on-one with the teacher—in order to improve their fluency. Students work in pairs, and each partner selects a passage to read aloud. Students begin by reading their passages silently. Then partners take turns being the reader or listener. Readers read their passages aloud three times. After the first reading, the listener does not provide feedback. After the second and third readings, the listener provides feedback to the reader.

Be sure to explain and model for students how to give one another constructive feedback. Model directly for students, using a volunteer reader. Tell students that comments such as, "I didn't know from your reading that this sentence was a question" or "I could understand you better if you slowed down and read louder" are more helpful than "Good job." Do a *fishbowl* exercise where the class observes a pair of readers and the class gives feedback on the pairs' feedback to one another. Once students are clear on how to give each other feedback, you will not have to repeat the modeling or fishbowl.

Reading to the Teacher—With small numbers of students in a class, it is possible to give regular attention on fluency to individual students. This gives you a clear sense of each student's strengths and weaknesses. Have students choose passages. Give them an opportunity to review them before they read them aloud to you. Give specific and constructive feedback on accuracy and prosody immediately after the reading. You can also use Echo Reading one-on-one to give students the opportunity for repetition.

Popcorn Reading—With popcorn reading, students take turns reading aloud. Students do not know who is going to be reading next, just as you do not know which kernel of corn will pop next. One student reads a sentence, a few sentences, or a paragraph. Then, he or she says "Popcorn, . . ." and calls another student's name. That student reads part of the passage and then *popcorns* someone else. Students stay on their toes, because they do not know who will be reading next.

Performance Reading—Many students enjoy working in pairs or small groups to dramatize the text they are reading. This strategy works well with texts that include a lot of dialogue. Assign students different roles, and have them practice the dialogue for their characters so that they are able to read their parts fluently and with expression from the text. Then have students perform for the class.

Fluency Tips for the Teacher

- Read and prepare the text before coming to class. It is easier to model fluency if you are already familiar with the text.
- Make sure students are familiar with the text before they begin to work on fluency. If students have already worked with the vocabulary and content of the text, they will struggle less with pronunciation and phrasing.

- You can use different fluency strategies with the same text. On one day, you might choose to use Echo Reading with a particular story; the next day, you might choose a passage from the same story and do Choral Reading. Remember that repetition is one of the keys to enhancing fluency.

- When pairing students, split the class into two groups according to reading ability. Have the top student of your more able readers work with the top student of your less able readers (conversely, have the low student of your best readers work with the lowest student of your lowest readers.) This may minimize frustration while still providing readers with support.

Keeping Track of Students' Progress

You will want to keep track of your students' reading progress. You can do this by informally recording each individual student's reading accuracy.

- Begin by choosing an unfamiliar passage of about 200 words in length that is at the student's reading level (perhaps from the next lesson in his or her student book or from the student books above or below that level.) Have the student read the passage aloud to you.

- On a separate copy of the same text, put a check mark over each word that is properly read. Each time a reader substitutes, omits, or inserts a word, count it as an error. If the student corrects herself, do not count those words as errors.

- Tally the errors and determine the percentage of words that were accurately read.

- Record a student's reading accuracy every few weeks in order to track progress.

Note: Running Records can be used to do a more thorough analysis of a student's reading and enable you to address individual challenges. You can go online to find explanations and examples of Running Records.

Choosing Happiness

Lesson Overview: (PAGE 5)

Theme

Have students read the lesson title on page 5 and tell them that the title introduces the lesson theme, Health. Invite students to make personal connections to the theme by mentioning their own values about health and how they create a healthy environment in their own homes.

Learning objectives

Read the learning objectives aloud and be sure students understand the outcome of each of the learning goals.

- *Learn about how people can make themselves happier.* Point out that the reading material is nonfiction. Its purpose is to give advice about how to become emotionally healthier. The vocabulary, comprehension, and writing exercises in this lesson are all related to the theme of health and wellness.
- *Learn to draw conclusions.*
- *Master the key vocabulary used in the article.*
- *Write suggestions for being happier.*

Preteach the vocabulary. (PAGE 5)

Read the key vocabulary words and their definitions to the students. Tell them that they will recognize all these words in the article.

- Distribute the Vocabulary Knowledge Rating Chart (Master 9) and have students individually rate each of the key vocabulary words.
- Preview particularly challenging words with students by listing each one on the board, modeling its use in a sentence, and having two or three students use the word in original sentences. Reframe student sentences that do not use the new words correctly.

You may wish to offer a mini-lesson on verbs as students read the respective parts of speech with the definitions of the vocabulary words. [See page 40 of this book for a mini-lesson on verbs. Use Master 3 or 4 to give students practice in recognizing verbs.]

Before You Read (PAGE 6)

Explain to students that active readers work to get the most from their reading. They use strategies to understand better what they read. Tell them that one good strategy for reading actively is to ask yourself questions before, during, and after reading to understand better the author and the meaning of the text.

Suggest that they take notes or write questions in the margins of their book to help them stay focused. Encourage them to include notes about whether they agree or disagree with what they are reading. Point out that the author offers many suggestions about how to develop behaviors that can lead to happiness. Writing notes in the margin may help students remember the suggestions that are most relevant to their lives.

As students begin to write answers to the questions for each element on page 6, have them read the respective Think About Its.

Set a purpose for reading. Explain that the title of the article helps the reader know what to expect. This title would interest a person who is worried about being unhappy. Use the Think About It to show that one purpose for reading is to find out how to make your life better. Point out that other readers may have different purposes. Ask students to describe their own thinking as they set a purpose for reading the article.

Ask yourself questions. Have students read the first paragraph of "How to Be Happy." Then have them read the second Think About It on page 6. Ask students to make a brief list of things they enjoy doing in their own lives. Ask what activities or people make them feel happy? Invite discussion about whether individuals can choose to be happy or if happiness comes from an outside source.

Reading the Article (PAGES 7–9)

Emphasize to students that they will read about a plan for happiness. They should expect to find tips and strategies for increasing happiness. Encourage students to highlight the tips that are most useful as they read.

Side-Column Vocabulary Remind students that the vocabulary words and phrases in the side column have been selected as important to the theme and content of the article. These words may be useful in the context of health problems and wellness, but they are not necessarily part of everyday language.

Mid-Passage Questions Some of the answers to the questions call on students' judgments, so there are not many right or wrong answers. Review students' written answers to assess whether they are getting meaning from the text. They should indicate in their answers that you are responsible for your own happiness. Ask students to share their feelings about practicing forgiveness and what would make them happier.

After You Read (PAGES 10–12)

Build a robust vocabulary. Ask students to check their answers in the answer keys in their books.

Think about your reading. Ask students to check their answers in the answer keys in their books. Ask additional questions to enrich the discussion so that students will be better able to write about solving emotional health problems. Here are some possible questions:

- What strategies does the author suggest for learning to forgive others? What does the author say will be the result of such actions? Do you have any experience with these strategies? Have they had a positive effect?

- In the discussion about money, the author says, "What research shows, though, is that after you have enough money to keep you out of poverty, more money doesn't bring happiness." What do you think the author is suggesting about the connection between money and happiness? Can you give an example of how money has not brought you happiness?

Extend the reading. Here are some additional activities to expand students' understanding.

- After reading the article, students may wish to make a set of goals for increasing their own happiness. Point out that goals should include as many details and be as concrete as possible. For example, a goal might be to walk for 15 minutes a day, three days a week.

- *For English Language Learners* Have students make a list of the feeling words in the article, such as *satisfied, grateful, bitterness, generous, happiness*. Discuss the shades of meaning among similar words. Invite students to give examples of when such feelings occur.

- Arrange students in pairs. Ask them to discuss whether they think the author is correct about how TV makes people less happy than other activities. Invite students to share their own experiences with watching TV. Then have pairs share their conclusions.

- Have students follow the suggestions in the article about writing a letter of forgiveness. You might want to keep the letters private or ask the class if they are willing to share their letters anonymously. Encourage them to use complete sentences and to express their ideas clearly. Review the correct format for letters with the class.

Use reading skills: Draw conclusions. Explain to students that when they draw conclusions, they rely on their own past experiences and their understanding of what they have read. The fact that most people have had some experience with unhappiness means that students should be able to relate to the discussion in the article and apply the ideas to solving their own problems. They use what they know about happiness to draw conclusions about how the suggestions will make a difference.

Use a graphic organizer. The conclusion diagram visually organizes past experiences and the conclusions based on them. It helps students to isolate areas where conclusions might be drawn.

Write About It (PAGES 13–14)

Write suggestions for becoming happier. Have students read the directions on page 13. Be sure they understand that they will write a paragraph that talks about things a friend might do to become happier.

Prewriting Point out that the graphic organizer, an idea map, helps to isolate important ideas to include in the paragraph. Tell students that thinking about smaller elements helps them analyze the problem and better organize their thinking about how to solve the problem. This will help them write their paragraphs in an organized manner so that their sentences logically follow each other. Encourage students to think and make notes about what the author suggests and their own ideas.

Thinking Beyond Reading Have students work with a partner or a small group to discuss the questions. The intent is for students to probe more deeply and to elaborate on the topic by addressing issues that did not arise when they were first thinking about ways to be happier. Encourage them to add ideas to their idea maps.

Write a draft. Have students write independently. Write on the board the following opening sentence *To be happy, you might want to do the following things*. Be sure that students understand that all the sentences in the paragraph must relate to the same main idea, in this case what your friend should do to become happier. Remind students to use the ideas in their idea maps to organize the different elements of their responses. These will be the details in their paragraphs. Encourage them to write their thoughts quickly and freely.

Revise and create a final draft. Remind students to use the Revising and Editing Checklist (Master 11) to guide them in revising their writing. Have students review each other's writing and give each other feedback on the parts of the paragraph that are logical, clear, and interesting, and the parts that need revision.

When students have finished revising their writing, use the Writing Rubric (Master 10) to evaluate it. Be sure you review your response with each student so he or she understands the strengths and weaknesses of this piece of writing. Have students date the writing and put the completed pieces in their writing portfolios.

Building Fluency

Identify small sections from "How to Be Happy." Tell students that they will use echo reading to read these sections aloud. Put students into groups of two. Give them time to read a passage silently 2–3 times to encourage their best oral reading. Remind them to pay attention to words that cause them to stumble. They will imitate your phrasing and intonation for each sentence. Remind students to use punctuation and typographic cues to add expression to their reading. Tell them that the goal is to read the passage as fluently as if they were just speaking.

Getting the Job

Lesson Overview: (PAGE 15)

Theme

Have students read the lesson title on page 15 and tell them that the title introduces the lesson theme, Work. Discuss the theme by having students make personal connections, telling about their jobs and what they did to get hired for their jobs.

Learning Objectives

Be sure students understand the outcome of each of the learning goals.

- *Learn about how to get a job.* Tell students that they will read the article either aloud or silently. Explain that the article will give advice about interviewing for a job.
- *Learn to identify main idea and details.*
- *Master the key vocabulary used in the article.*
- *Write a thank-you letter to a job interviewer.*

Preteach the vocabulary. (PAGE 15)

Read the key vocabulary words and their definitions to the students. Tell them that they will recognize all these words in the article.

- Distribute the Vocabulary Knowledge Rating Chart (Master 9) and have students individually rate each of the key vocabulary words.
- Preview particularly challenging words with students by listing each one on the board, modeling its use in a sentence, and having two or three students use the word in original sentences. Reframe student sentences that do not use the new words correctly.

You may wish to offer a mini-lesson on adjectives as students read the respective parts of speech with the definitions of the vocabulary words. [See page 41 of this book for a mini-lesson on adjectives. Use Master 5 or 6 to give students practice in recognizing adjectives.]

Before You Read (PAGE 16)

Explain to students that active readers work to get the most from their reading. They use strategies to understand better what they read. Explain that good readers will ask questions before, during, and after reading to understand better the meaning of the text. Suggest that they make notes or write questions in the margins of their books to help them stay focused. Encourage them to include notes about whether they agree or disagree with what they are reading.

Explain that as they read this article, they will find that it is about how to prepare for and behave at a job interview. Remind students to ask questions about the information as they read. Then they should look for answers in the text.

As students begin to write answers to the questions for each element on page 16, have them read aloud the respective Think About Its.

Set a purpose for reading. Ask questions to help students identify an appropriate purpose for reading an informational article. For example, *Do you think you will be entertained? Do you think you will find job listings? Do you think you will find out what a company is like to work for?* By eliminating other purposes, students should be able to narrow down a purpose for reading this article.

Ask yourself questions. Use the Think About It to begin a discussion about the position of the interviewer. Elicit responses to the questions, and explain how questioning during reading helps the reader to focus. Invite students to use sticky notes on the book to jot down questions and answers as they read.

Reading the Article (PAGES 17–19)

Emphasize to students that from the beginning of the article, it is clear that it will focus on what to do before, during, and after the interview, not on landing it. It will help the reader become prepared and feel confident during an interview.

Side-Column Vocabulary   Remind students that the vocabulary words and phrases in the side column have been selected as important to the theme and content of the article. These words may be useful in the context of job interviews, but they are not necessarily part of everyday language.

Mid-Passage Questions   Some of the answers to the questions are largely students' opinions, so there are not many right or wrong answers. Review students' written answers to assess whether they are getting meaning from the text. They should indicate in their answers that preparing for an interview includes more than just getting there on time.

After You Read (PAGES 20–22)

Build a robust vocabulary.   Ask students to check their answers in the answer keys in their books.

Think about your reading.   Ask students to check their answers in the answer keys in their books. Ask additional questions to enrich the discussion so that students will be better able to write about a successful job interview. Here are some possible questions:

- A good reader notices causes and effects. What does the author suggest would be the effect of wearing sneakers, baggy jeans, and a sweatshirt to a job interview? How else does the author suggest that the interviewee can control his or her effect on the interviewer?

- Why do you think it is important not to speak negatively about your previous work experiences? What generalizations do you think an interviewer could make about someone who tells negative stories about an earlier job?

Extend the reading.   Here are some additional activities to expand students' understanding.

- Have each student find a person who has been on several interviews and ask him or her about them. Find out which of the specific suggestions from the text were important.

- With your family, make a list of the qualities and skills you have that would make you a good worker. Include skills that may not be related to work, such as the ability to organize many family members for an outing or project. Think about which of the skills would be most desirable to an employer.

- *For English Language Learners*   These idiomatic phrases may pose problems to some readers: *good fit for the job, how much you will make, work history, take over the conversation, good hire, one-way street.* Write them on the board. Find each phrase in the article and explain its meaning in the context of the reading.

- After thinking about the needs of an employer, have students write a first draft of a résumé. Include information about school, past employers, and details about each job that would be interesting to a potential employer.

Use reading skills: Identify main idea and details. Finding the main idea of an article or paragraph means thinking about the overall point the author is making. Some students may make a list of the details outlined in the article. Then they look at how all the details fit together to create a main idea. In some cases, the main idea of one paragraph becomes one of the details that explain the main idea of the article or section as a whole. Practice finding main ideas in small paragraphs. Then use the same skill to find the main idea of a section of longer text.

Use a graphic organizer.   The main idea and details web visually organizes ideas in part of the article. It gives the main idea and asks students to identify details that support the idea.

Write About It (PAGES 23–24)

Write a thank-you letter.   Have students read the directions on page 23 and be sure they understand that they will write a thank-you letter following an imagined interview.

Prewriting   Explain that the main idea of a thank-you letter is to show appreciation for the interviewer's time and to remind him or her of why you are right for the job. Have students begin by imagining an interview that they will refer to in the letter. This may be a real life interview or one that they wish they could get for a desirable job.

Thinking Beyond Reading   Have students work with a partner or a small group to brainstorm details that would be important to include in the letter. Partners should suggest strengths and experiences that could influence the decision of the interviewer. Encourage students to add ideas to their webs.

Write a draft.   Have students write independently. Suggest that they divide the letter into two paragraphs. The first should be the thank-you portion. The second should give details about their own strengths for the job. Remind students of correct letter-writing format with the return address and date at the top, the interviewer's address below that, a salutation, the body of the letter, then the closing words, and the signature. Remind students to use the ideas in their webs to identify relevant details for their letters. While drafting, students should not be concerned with spelling or punctuation. Encourage them to write their thoughts quickly and freely.

Revise and create a final draft.   Remind students to use the Revising and Editing Checklist (Master 11) to guide them in making revisions to their writing. Explain that an interviewer will demand correct spelling and punctuation, so accuracy is important. Have students review each other's writing and give feedback on the parts of the letter that are logical, clear, and interesting, and the parts of the letter that need revision.

When students have finished revising their writing, use the Writing Rubric (Master 10) to evaluate it. Be sure you review your response with each student so he or she understands the strengths and weaknesses of this piece of writing. Have students date the writing and put the completed pieces in their writing portfolios.

Building Fluency

Identify small sections from "The Job Interview." Tell students that they will use paired reading to read these sections aloud. Put students into groups of two. Give them time to read a passage silently 2–3 times to encourage their best oral reading. Partners take turns being the reader or listener. After the first reading, the listener does not provide feedback. After the second and third readings, the listener provides feedback to the reader. Remind students to pay attention to words that cause them to stumble and to read for the author's message. Their goal is to read the passage as fluently as if they were just speaking.

The Stepfamily

Lesson Overview: (PAGE 25)

Theme

Have students read the lesson title on page 25 and tell them that the title introduces the lesson theme, Family. Discuss the theme by having students make personal connections, telling about families that they know and how they work to stay together and happy.

Learning objectives

Read the learning objectives aloud and be sure students understand the outcome of each of the learning goals.

- *Read a story about family members trying to get along with each other.* Point out that the story is fiction. The conflicts in the story are written to provoke a discussion and to show a resolution to a family conflict.
- *Learn to compare and contrast.*
- *Master the key vocabulary used in the story.*
- *Write an e-mail about a family's problem and how the problem was resolved.*

Preteach the vocabulary. (PAGE 25)

Read the key vocabulary words and their definitions to the students. Tell them that they will recognize all these words in the story.

- Distribute the Vocabulary Knowledge Rating Chart (Master 9) and have students individually rate each of the key vocabulary words.
- Preview particularly challenging words with students by listing each one on the board, modeling its use in a sentence, and having two or three students use the word in original sentences. Reframe student sentences that do not use the new words correctly.

You may wish to offer a mini-lesson on adverbs as students read the respective parts of speech with the definitions of the vocabulary words. [See page 42 of this book for a mini-lesson on adverbs. Use Master 7 or 8 to give students practice in recognizing adverbs.]

Before You Read (PAGE 26)

Explain to students that good readers ask themselves questions before, during, and after reading to understand better the author and the meaning of the text. Suggest that they take notes or write questions in the margins of their book to help them stay focused. Encourage them to include notes about whether they agree or disagree with what they are reading.

As students begin to write answers to the questions for each element on page 26, have them read the respective Think About Its.

Predict what will happen. As students answer the questions, remind them that the title of the story offers a clue to its main idea. Point out that the family relationships give some indication of the power structure of the family. For example, the grown-ups will have more power to control the family than the child does.

Ask yourself questions. Remind students that good readers ask questions to get more out of a story. Use the Think About It to elicit discussion about what questions are relevant to ask at the beginning of a reading assignment.

Reading the Story (PAGES 27–29)

Emphasize to students that their purpose for reading is to find out what the conflict is between the two main characters, Doris and Gilly. Highlighting phrases that show how the relationship is in conflict will keep readers involved in the story.

Side-Column Vocabulary Remind students that the vocabulary words and phrases in the side column have been selected as important to the theme and content of the story. These words may be useful in the context of family conflict, but they are not necessarily part of everyday language.

Mid-Passage Questions   Some of the answers to the questions call on students' judgments, so there are not many right or wrong answers. Review students' written answers to assess whether they are getting meaning from the text. They should correctly indicate that Gilly is unhappy about Doris's many rules. They should also understand that Gilly's plan to hurt Doris involves lies and revenge, or "payback." Students should understand that Frank initially believes his daughter.

After You Read (PAGES 30–32)

Build a robust vocabulary.   Ask students to check their answers in the answer keys in their books.

Think about your reading.   Ask students to check their answers in the answer keys in their books. Ask additional questions to enrich the discussion so that students will be better able to write about solving family problems. Here are some possible questions:

- Although the author does not give details, how long do you think the conflict has been going on between the three family members? Have students think about the causes that may have led to the conflict.

- A good reader reads "between the lines." What lie was Gilly telling her father about Doris? What did Frank believe when Gilly gave him the information?

   Extend the reading.   Here are some additional activities to expand the students' understanding.

   - Have students work in groups of four to read the story aloud. Assign one character to each student with the fourth student reading the part of the narrator/author. Have students read with expression in the tone they think the speaker would use. Allow time to prepare.

   - *For English Language Learners* Explain that an adverb is a word that tells about an action.

Point out the adverbs in the story, such as *cheerfully, clearly, defiantly, sharply, wearily, hesitantly, dejectedly,* and *sharply.* Have students find the verb that each adverb modifies.

- Recognizing that a conflict cannot exist without two parties, challenge students to perform one act of kindness toward their family members at home. Have them share the effects of the act with their classmates, noting whether the action produced positive or negative results.

- Discuss whether the conclusion of the story is realistic. Have students talk about or write what may have taken place between the characters from when the family first started going to the therapist to when Gilly asked Doris to go shopping.

Use reading skills: Compare and contrast.   Share with students that there are transition words that can help them identify when something is being compared or contrasted. Words such as *also, and, as, like, likewise, similarly,* and *too* are often used to show a comparison. Words that are often used to show a contrast are *although, however, in contrast, nevertheless, on the other hand, but, still,* and *yet.*

Use a graphic organizer.   A graphic organizer can help students analyze narrative or informative text in order to understand it better. Often it can serve as a planning tool to organize a writer's thinking about a text. The visual relationships among the ideas in the text help the reader see the way the text works. In this case the chart shows how things change in the story.

Write About It (PAGES 33–34)

Write an e-mail.   Have students read the directions at the top of page 33 and be sure they understand that they will write an e-mail about a family conflict.

Prewriting   Point out to students that the e-mail should focus on a conflict that has already been resolved. Suggest that students make a chart similar to the one in the book to analyze how the conflict changed over time. Encourage students to think and make notes about the problem and possible solutions as comprehensively as possible.

Thinking Beyond Reading Have students work with a partner or a small group to discuss the questions. The intent is for students to probe more deeply and to elaborate on the topic by addressing issues that did not arise when they were first thinking about the family conflict. Encourage them to add ideas to their charts and improve their notes.

Write a draft. Have students write independently. Write on the board the following opening sentence *All families go through periods of conflict, and my friend's family is no different.* Students should structure their e-mails chronologically, beginning with the events that led to the original conflict. Remind students to use the ideas in their charts to help them organize their e-mails. Encourage them to write their thoughts quickly and freely.

Revise and create a final draft. Remind students to use the Revising and Editing Checklist (Master 11) to guide them in revising their writing. Have students review each other's writing and give each other feedback on the parts of the e-mail that are logical, clear, and interesting, and the parts that need revision.

When students have finished revising their writing, use the Writing Rubric (Master 10) to evaluate it. Be sure you review your response with each student so he or she understands the strengths and weaknesses of this piece of writing. Have students date the writing and put the completed pieces in their writing portfolios.

Building Fluency

Identify small sections from "Blending In." Tell students that they will use echo reading to read these sections aloud. Put students into groups of two. Give them time to read a passage silently 2–3 times to encourage their best oral reading. Remind them to pay attention to words that cause them to stumble. They will imitate your phrasing and intonation for each sentence. Remind students to use punctuation and typographic cues to add expression to their reading. Tell them that the goal is to read the passage as fluently as if they were just speaking.

Living in a Community

Lesson Overview: (PAGE 35)

Theme

Have students read the lesson title on page 35, and tell them that the title introduces the lesson theme, Community. Discuss the theme by having students tell the positive things that make their own community a special place.

Learning Objectives

Be sure students understand the outcome of each of the learning goals.

- *Read a story about people who changed their community.* Point out that the story is fiction and the author makes up the characters and dialogue. Although some students may not be able to relate to starting a garden, they may be able to understand the frustration of living in a run-down community.

- *Learn to identify cause and effect.*

- *Master the key vocabulary used in the story.*

- *Write a personal narrative about something you did that you were proud of and that helped someone out.*

Preteach the vocabulary. (PAGE 35)

Read the key vocabulary words and their definitions to students. Tell them that they will recognize all these words in the story.

- Distribute the Vocabulary Knowledge Rating Chart (Master 9) and have students individually rate each of the key vocabulary words.

- Preview particularly challenging words with students by listing each one on the board, modeling its use in a sentence, and having two or three students use the word in original sentences. Reframe student sentences that do not use the new words correctly.

You may wish to offer a mini-lesson on adjectives as students read the respective parts of speech with the definitions of the vocabulary words. [See page 41 of this book for a mini-lesson on adjectives. Use Master 5 or 6 to give students practice in recognizing adjectives.]

Before You Read (PAGE 36)

Explain to students that active readers get more out of their reading. Tell them that active reading is like talking back to the page. Active readers react to what they read, which makes them more involved with the story. Getting involved helps readers remember more of what they read.

As students begin to write answers to the questions for each element on page 36, have them read the respective Think About Its.

Make predictions. Use the Think About Its to encourage students to make prediction before they start reading. Identify the character Jamal, and invite students to visualize his age, race, appearance, and personality. Have them predict what he might do in the story.

Summarize. Remind students to summarize each section of the story after they read it, jotting down what happened in their own words.

Reading the Story (PAGES 37–39)

Emphasize to students that reading to find out why Jamal is angry gives them a purpose for reading the passage. It is a question to answer as they read. Highlighting phrases that are clues to Jamal's feelings is a strategy that will keep them involved in the story.

Side-Column Vocabulary Remind students that the vocabulary words and phrases in the side column have been selected as important to the theme and content of the story. These words may be useful in the context of community gardening, but they are not necessarily part of everyday language.

Mid-Passage Questions The answers to the questions are largely students' opinions, so there are not many right or wrong answers. Review students' written answers to assess whether they are getting meaning from the text. They should indicate in their answers that Jamal is upset that his community does not care about its spaces. They should recognize that Lakeesha suggests building a community garden to solve the problem. They should understand the steps in setting up a community garden and the discouragement that Jamal and Lakeesha feel when they begin the garden.

After You Read (PAGES 40–42)

Build a robust vocabulary. Ask students to check their answers in the answer keys in their books.

Think about your reading. Ask students to check their answers in the answer keys in their books. Ask additional questions to enrich the discussion so that students will be better able to write about how the characters feel about solving the problem in their community.

- A good reader reads "between the lines." How much experience do you think Jamal and Lakeesha have with gardening? What clues in the story help form your opinion? What resources are available in Jamal's community to make his idea a reality?

- At several points in the story, Jamal and Lakeesha feel like giving up on the project. What character traits do they have that keep them going? Why don't they quit?

Extend the reading. Here are some additional activities to expand students' understanding.

- Explain that each story has a theme, or overriding message. Sometimes stories can have several themes. Ask students to brainstorm ideas about the theme of "Something Good." Some may focus on the character development and point out that helping oneself can often lead to helping others. Other themes include the healing powers of nature, the ways people help make things better, and so on.

- *For English Language Learners* Point out several incomplete sentences in the story, such as, "Nothing but junk." "Place is a disgrace." "Know where they came from?" Explain that these are not complete sentences and that sometimes authors write dialogue that mimics the way people really speak. Have students supply the missing parts of the sentences, making sure that they understand the meaning of the dialogue and the reason for the author's technique.

- Discuss the ways that the garden in the story became a special place. Reread the paragraph about what community members did to participate in the garden. Ask students to tell why these actions made the space different from what it had been.

Use reading skills: Identify cause and effect. Effective readers recognize how causes and effects connect the events in a story. For example, Jamal was motivated to make a change in his community after a bottle almost hit him in the head. Authors often build in special meaning when they explain the causes and effects within the plot. Such a technique allows them to make an important point or emphasize a main idea. Recognizing causes and effects is an important life skill as well. By understanding that no event occurs without a cause, students can begin to see patterns in their own lives and take steps to control events.

Use a graphic organizer. The cause and effect chart visually organizes the events of the story. The chart helps the reader separate the reasons for and results of the story's events.

Write About It (PAGES 43–44)

Write a personal narrative. Have students read the directions on page 43. Be sure they understand that they will write a personal narrative that describes the steps they took to accomplish a project they are proud of.

Prewriting Have students brainstorm projects they have undertaken. Tell students to use the graphic organizer, a cause and effect chart, to help them break down their ideas into smaller parts. Encourage students to think and make notes about their projects and the tasks they accomplished to make them happen. Encourage students to add additional steps or details to their charts if they need to.

Thinking Beyond Reading Have students work with a partner or a small group to discuss the questions. The intent is for students to probe more deeply and to elaborate on the topic by addressing issues that did not arise when they were first thinking about the project they have chosen to discuss. Encourage them to add ideas to their cause and effect charts.

Write a draft. Have students write independently. Write on the board the following topic sentence *Helping my friend meant following some important steps one at a time.* Be sure that students understand that all the sentences in the paragraph must relate to the same main idea, and be arranged in chronological order. Remind students to use the ideas in their cause and effect charts to organize the steps in their processes. While drafting, students should not be concerned with spelling or punctuation. Encourage them to write their thoughts quickly and freely.

Revise and create a final draft. Remind students to use the Revising and Editing Checklist (Master 11) to guide them in revising their writing. Have students review each other's writing and give each other feedback on the parts of the paragraph that are logical, clear, and interesting, and the parts of the paragraph that need revision.

When students have finished revising their writing, use the Writing Rubric (Master 10) to evaluate it. Be sure you review your response with each student so he or she understands the strengths and weaknesses of this piece of writing. Have students date the writing and put the completed pieces in their writing portfolios.

Building Fluency

Identify small sections from "Something Good." Tell students that they will use choral reading to read these sections aloud. Give them time to read a passage silently 2–3 times to encourage the best oral reading. In order to set and maintain the pace, read along with the students. Identify words that cause the students to stumble. They will imitate the phrasing and intonation that you model. Remind students to use punctuation and typographic cues to add expression to their reading. Tell them that the goal is to read the passage as fluently as if they were just speaking.

Learn a Trade

Lesson Overview: (PAGE 45)

Theme

Have students read the lesson title on page 45, and tell them that the title introduces the lesson theme, School and Education. Discuss the theme by having students make personal connections, telling what kind of schooling they've had and the kind of schooling they still want.

Learning objectives

Be sure students understand the outcome of each of the learning goals.

- *Learn about trade schools.* Point out that this article offers advice. It is nonfiction, and it tells the benefits and strengths of vocational education, as well as some of the issues to watch for when choosing a school.
- *Learn to make inferences from what you read and what you know.*
- *Master the key vocabulary used in the article.*
- *Write a summary of the article about choosing a trade school.*

Preteach the vocabulary. (PAGE 45)

Read the key vocabulary words and their definitions to the students. Tell them that they will recognize all these words in the article.

- Distribute the Vocabulary Knowledge Rating Chart (Master 9) and have students individually rate each of the key vocabulary words.
- Preview particularly challenging words with students by listing each one on the board and modeling its use in a sentence. Have two or three students use the words in original sentences. Reframe student sentences that do not use the new words correctly.

You may wish to offer a mini-lesson on nouns as students read the respective parts of speech with the definitions of the vocabulary words. [See page 39 of this book for a mini-lesson on nouns. Use Master 1 or 2 to give students practice in recognizing nouns.]

Before You Read (PAGE 46)

Tell students that the more active they are as readers, the more they will get out of reading. When they read actively, they think about what they are reading and use different strategies—such as asking themselves questions—to understand the ideas they are reading. Active readers "talk back" to the writer. They think of questions they want answered as they read.

Remind students that as they begin to read this article, they might ask if a vocational school is right for them. They may have questions about choosing a vocational school and wonder if attending one will help them get a good job. Tell them to keep those questions in mind as they read the article.

As students begin to write answers to the questions for each element on page 46, have them read the respective Think About Its.

Set a purpose for reading. Tell students that even though they may not be interested in a trade school at this time, the information could be useful in the future as their job interests change or when they are asked for advice by friends or family members. Setting a purpose of finding out more will help them be more active readers. Use the Think About It to elicit a discussion of what jobs may be available after special training.

Ask yourself questions. Recognize that some students may have incorrect preconceived notions about vocational schools and that by asking questions, they may be able to clarify many issues. Invite students to share their concerns or perceptions about vocational schools and to form them into questions that may be answered by the article.

Reading the Article (PAGES 47–49)

Emphasize to students that they are reading to find out how vocational schools attract students in their advertisements. This is a question to think about as they read. Highlighting phrases that are clues to advertising strategies will keep them involved in the article.

Side-Column Vocabulary Remind students that the vocabulary words and phrases in the side column have been selected as important to the theme and content of the story. These words may be useful in the context of vocational and for-profit schools, but they are not necessarily part of everyday language.

Mid-Passage Questions Some of the answers to the questions call on students' judgments, so there are not many right or wrong answers. Review students' written answers to assess whether they are getting meaning from the text. Their answers should show some understanding of how a for–profit vocational school educates students for certain career paths. Student questions should show understanding that schools may not be what they appear to be.

After You Read (PAGES 50–52)

Build a robust vocabulary. Ask students to check their answers in the answer keys in their books.

Think about your reading. Ask students to check their answers in the answer keys in their books. Ask additional questions to enrich the discussion so that students will be better able to write about vocational schools. Here are some possible questions:

- A good reader reads "between the lines." Why does the article suggest that some schools make false claims about what they can do for their students? Encourage students to read and interpret the paragraph about for-profit businesses.

- Drawing conclusions means using information you already know and combining it with information

you read. What can you tell about a school if its students do not get good jobs or if they do not pass the licensing tests? What conclusions can you draw about the school?

Extend the reading. Here are some additional activities to expand students' understanding.

- Students may enjoy sharing their own experiences with vocational schools. Invite them to tell what they know and to explain whether they or any friend of theirs has been misled by the promises of a vocational school. To follow up on the discussion, find the passage in the article that suggests how such problems might have been avoided.

- *For English Language Learners* Have students reread the fourth paragraph of the article on page 47. Point out the job titles in the paragraph with which they may not be familiar. Explain how the government in this country controls training for certain jobs by issuing licenses. Point out that the purpose of this licensing is to ensure safety and adequate skills among the people on the job.

- At home, have students take notes on TV advertisements for vocational schools. Have them note what promises a school makes that could be misinformation. Invite students to share their notes with the class and to evaluate the advertisements based on the suggestions in the article.

- Point out that many students have difficulty in school because they do not feel that the material they are learning is relevant. Ask students to consider whether vocational school work is different from regular academic schoolwork because it directly trains students for work in the real world. Discuss the similarities and differences between the two types of schools.

Use reading skills: Make inferences. Remind students that an inference is a combination of what they read with information they already know. Point out that in this article, the author leaves some ideas unstated, allowing the reader to infer the point of the writing. A reader must be actively engaged to pick up all the author's ideas. Explain that making inferences is a life skill since we gather information from many sources and make inferences about the truth of each situation.

Use a graphic organizer. The inferences diagram allows students to write what they already know and combine it with new information from the text to infer something from the reading.

Write About It (PAGES 53–54)

Write a summary. Have students read the directions on page 53. Be sure they understand that they will write a summary of the article about vocational schools.

Prewriting Point out that the graphic organizer, an idea map, helps isolate important points to include in the paragraph. Remind students that a summary includes the main points of an article. It leaves out details and many explanations, and should touch on all the major points of the article. Encourage them to write notes in their idea web in order to organize their writing.

Thinking Beyond Reading Have students work with a partner or a small group to discuss the questions. The intent is for students to probe more deeply and to come up with more questions and concerns about trade schools.

Write a draft. Have students write independently. Write the following opening sentence on the board: *Making a choice about a vocational school involves doing a lot of homework.* Be sure that students understand that all the sentences in the paragraph must relate to the same main idea, in this case how to choose the right school. Remind students to use the ideas in their idea webs to organize the different elements of their responses. Encourage students to write their thoughts quickly and freely.

Revise and create a final draft. Remind students to use the Revising and Editing Checklist (Master 11) to guide them in revising their writing. Have students review each other's writing and give each other feedback on how the summary can be narrowed to eliminate any unnecessary details.

When students have finished revising their writing, use the Writing Rubric (Master 10) to evaluate it. Be sure you review your response with each student so he or she understands the strengths and weaknesses of this piece of writing. Have students date the writing and put the completed pieces in their writing portfolios.

Building Fluency

Identify small sections from "Is Vocational School Right For Me?" Tell students that they will use paired reading to read these sections aloud. Put students into groups of two. Give them time to read a passage silently 2–3 times to encourage their best oral reading. Partners take turns being the reader or listener. After the first reading, the listener does not provide feedback. After the second and third readings, the listener provides feedback to the reader. Remind students to pay attention to words that cause them to stumble and to read for the author's message. Their goal is to read the passage as fluently as if they were just speaking.

Trial by Jury

Lesson Overview: (PAGE 55)

Theme

Have students read the lesson title on page 55 and tell them that the title introduces the lesson theme, Civics and Government. Discuss the theme by having students make personal connections, telling how they get involved in their own communities and how they relate to their local government. Ask them to tell about their volunteer work or service projects, and whether they ever attend town or school board meetings. Ask them if they have ever been called for jury duty.

Learning Objectives

Be sure students understand the outcome of each of the learning goals.

- *Read a story about a person who serves on a jury.* Point out that this is fiction and that the author uses suspense and mystery to capture the attention of the reader.
- *Learn to synthesize, or put together, ideas.*
- *Master the key vocabulary used in the story.*
- *Write a paragraph that explains how the jury reached its verdict.*

Preteach the vocabulary. (PAGE 55)

Read the key vocabulary words and their definitions to students. Tell them that they will recognize all these words in the story.

- Distribute the Vocabulary Knowledge Rating Chart (Master 9) and have students individually rate each of the key vocabulary words.
- Preview particularly challenging words with students by listing each one on the board and modeling its use in a sentence. Have two or three students use the word in original sentences. Reframe student sentences that do not use the new words correctly.

You may wish to offer a mini-lesson on adverbs as students read the respective parts of speech with the definitions of the vocabulary words. [See page 42 of this book for a mini-lesson on adverbs. Use Master 7 or 8 to give students practice in recognizing adverbs.]

Before You Read (PAGE 56)

Explain to students that active readers get more out of their reading. Tell them that active reading is like talking back to the page. Active readers react to what they read, which makes them more involved with the story. Getting involved helps readers remember more of what they read.

As students begin to write answers to the questions for each element on page 56, have them read aloud the respective Think About Its.

Use what you know. Use the Think About It to elicit a discussion about students' personal experiences with a courtroom. Encourage students to compare their own experiences with TV courtrooms, telling how the reality is different from television scenes. Students are likely to say that the TV courtrooms are cleaner and that the people are more fashionably dressed on TV, but for the most part, the seriousness of both kinds of courtrooms is similar. Point out that real court cases take many hours and involve many witnesses—that they are not completed within the few minutes allowed during a television program.

Reread what you don't understand. Draw attention to sections of the lesson that offer vocabulary support, including definitions listed in the margins, the list of vocabulary words at the beginning of the lesson, and context clues within the text. Encourage students to note challenging passages and ask for additional help from a fluent English speaker or from you.

Reading the Story (PAGES 57–59)

Emphasize to students that they will be reading to find out how a jury reaches a verdict during a trial. This is the purpose for reading the passage and is the question to keep in mind as they read. Encourage students to highlight sentences that help them understand the progress of the trial and keep them involved in the story.

Side-Column Vocabulary Remind students that the vocabulary words and phrases in the side column have been selected as important to the theme and content of the story. These words may be useful in the context of the justice system and jury trials, but they are not necessarily part of everyday language.

Mid-Passage Questions The answers to the questions are largely students' opinions, so there are not many right or wrong answers. Review students' written answers to assess whether they are getting meaning from the text. They should indicate in their answers their own experiences with jury summonses and their predictions about the outcome of the trial. Their explanations of who they think is telling the truth in the story should be based on details from the text. Finally, ask them to share their feelings about the jury's decision.

After You Read (PAGES 60–62)

Build a robust vocabulary. Ask students to check their answers in the answer keys in their books.

Think about your reading. Ask students to check their answers in the answer keys in their books. Ask additional questions to enrich the discussion so that students will be better able to write about the court and jury systems. Here are some possible questions:

- Point out these sentences near the end of the story, "If we have reasonable doubt about whether he did it, he's innocent. That's the law." Do you think the jury should have had reasonable doubt about Kevin's guilt? What testimony is probably missing from the story that would have erased all doubt from

the case? Students should recognize that there are several days of the case that are not accounted for in the story. These require them to read "between the lines." Have them speculate on who else may have testified and affected the final verdict.

- Explain that the ending of a story sometimes has as much impact as the whole work. What has the author done at the end to call the jury's decision into question? Why did the author cast a shadow of doubt in Kaycee's reaction to the trial? What effect does the doubt have on the reader's understanding of the fairness of the trial?

Extend the reading. Here are some additional activities to expand students' understanding.

- Students may enjoy writing a scene for the story in which the attorneys ask questions of Janice's old boyfriend. Challenge them to invent answers that would show Kevin to be guilty or not guilty, depending on the student's opinion of Kevin's role in the crime. Ask students to share their work by reading it aloud.

- *For English Language Learners* Point out that in this country a jury is made up of citizens from the county in which the crime was committed. Citizens are called to report to a courtroom for duty. However, not every citizen called will sit on a jury. Explain that sometimes, a citizen has past experience that will unfairly bias his or her judgment about a case. In this situation, the citizen is not asked to be on the jury. Point out the passage where the court official asked if anyone had been the victim of a violent crime. Discuss with students how such an experience might make a person judge Kevin before hearing the evidence against him.

- Have students read the newspaper at home to find stories about court cases. Have them highlight passages in the news articles that offer details about the courtroom, the testimony of witnesses, and the verdicts in the cases. Invite students to share their newspaper stories with the class.

Use reading skills: Synthesize. Experienced readers gather information as they read and integrate it to understand an event. This is called synthesizing. Point out to students that we synthesize information every day by offering an example: Suppose there was a large and angry neighborhood meeting in your community. By talking to several people, you get several versions of what happened. You synthesize what you have learned to come up with a better understanding of what happened.

Use a graphic organizer. The chart visually organizes different aspects of how the jury reached a verdict. It helps the writer organize the steps in the order they happen.

Write About It (PAGES 63–64)

Write an explanation. Have students read the directions on page 63 and be sure they understand that they will write an explanation of how the jury reached its verdict.

Prewriting Have students fill in the idea web for this writing assignment. To gather information, have them reread the story and include all the points the author includes. Point out that the graphic organizer breaks the problem and its solutions into smaller parts. Explain to students that thinking about smaller elements helps them to analyze the problem and better organize their thinking about each step in the process of reaching a verdict. This collection of details will help them explain the jury's work.

Thinking Beyond Reading Have students work with a partner or a small group to discuss the questions. The intent is for students to probe more deeply and to elaborate on the topic by addressing issues that did not arise when they were first thinking about how the jury reached its verdict. Encourage students to add ideas to their webs.

Write a draft. Have students write independently. Write on the board the following topic sentence: *The jury reached its verdict by looking at a number of things.* Be sure that students understand that all the sentences in the paragraph must relate to the same main idea, in this case why the jury reached its verdict. Remind students to use the ideas in their webs to organize the different elements of their responses. These will be the details in their paragraphs. Encourage them to write their thoughts quickly and freely.

Revise and create a final draft. Remind students to use the Revising and Editing Checklist (Master 11) to guide them in making revisions to their writing. Have students review each other's writing and give each other feedback on the parts of the paragraph that are logical, clear, and interesting, and the parts of the paragraph that need revision.

When students have finished revising their writing, use the Writing Rubric (Master 10) to evaluate it. Be sure you review your response with each student so he or she understands the strengths and weaknesses of this piece of writing. Have students date the writing and put the completed pieces in their writing portfolios.

Building Fluency

Identify small sections from "The Verdict." Tell students that they will use echo reading to read these sections aloud. Put students into groups of two. Give them time to read a passage silently 2–3 times to encourage their best oral reading. Remind them to pay attention to words that cause them to stumble. They will imitate your phrasing and intonation for each sentence. Remind students that you will use punctuation and typographic cues to add expression to the reading. Explain to them that the goal is to read the passage as fluently as if they were just speaking.

Staying Fit

Lesson Overview: (PAGE 65)

Theme

Have students read the lesson title on page 65 and tell them that the title introduces the lesson theme, Sports and Recreation. Discuss the theme by having students share their own fitness routines including the exercises, sports, and other physical activities they participate in.

Learning Objectives

Be sure students understand the outcome of each of the learning goals.

- *Learn about the benefits of walking.* Tell students that this article gives instructions for walking as a form of exercise. Point out that the vocabulary and writing assignments relate to the theme of fitness.
- *Learn to make inferences.*
- *Master the key vocabulary used in the article.*
- *Write a description of a good fitness walk.*

Preteach the vocabulary. (PAGE 65)

Read the key vocabulary words and their definitions to the students. Tell them that they will recognize all these words in the article.

- Distribute the Vocabulary Knowledge Rating Chart (Master 9) and have students individually rate each of the key vocabulary words.
- Preview particularly challenging words with students by listing each one on the board, modeling its use in a sentence, and having two or three students use the word in original sentences. Reframe student sentences that do not use the new words correctly.

You may wish to offer a mini-lesson on verbs as students read the respective parts of speech with the definitions of the vocabulary words. [See page 40 of this book for a mini-lesson on verbs. Use Master 3 or 4 to give students practice in recognizing verbs.]

Before You Read (PAGE 66)

Review with students what it means to be an active reader. Point out that active readers ask themselves, "What do I know that will help me read between the lines? What answers do I think I will find?" Explain that the article is about walking as a strategy for good health. Many students may have experience with a fitness program. Such background knowledge can help them understand the article.

As students begin to write answers to the questions for each element on page 66, have them read the respective Think About Its.

Make predictions. In answering the questions, many students are likely to discuss their own experiences walking. They may also recognize that walking improves a person's outlook on life, thus improving mental health.

Make personal connections with the topic. Use the Think About It to start a discussion about walking for fitness. Invite students to share their personal experiences with the class. Point out that making a personal connection with reading material makes a person a better reader since he or she will remember the material longer.

Reading the Article (PAGES 67–69)

Emphasize to students that their purpose for reading is to find out how one of the simplest things you can do may also be one of the best for your health. This is a question to keep in mind as they read.

Side-Column Vocabulary Remind students that the vocabulary words and phrases in the side column have been selected as important to the theme and content of the article. These words may be useful in the context of fitness or walking, but they are not necessarily part of everyday language.

Mid-Passage Questions Some of the answers to the questions call on students' judgments, so there are not many right or wrong answers. Review students' written answers to assess whether they are getting meaning from the text. They should indicate that people with diabetes can keep their blood sugar low by walking and that walking can help burn calories, which, in turn, keeps weight down. They should recognize the suggestions about walking shoes and the importance of stretching before walking.

After You Read (PAGES 70–72)

Build a robust vocabulary. Ask students to check their answers in the answer keys in their books.

Think about your reading. Ask students to check their answers in the answer keys in their books. Ask additional questions to enrich the discussion so that students will be better able to write about beginning a walking program. Here are some possible questions:

- Good readers make judgments as they read. Ask students what they think are the best reasons for walking. Point out that the article gives a variety of reasons, but some may be more convincing than others. Ask students to evaluate the author's list and tell which reasons are strongest.

- Point out that the author suggests that walking is a solution to many problems. Ask students to identify other problems that walking can solve. Discuss how the same author might write a problem/solution article about each of those cases.

Extend the reading. Here are some additional activities to expand students' understanding.

- At home, have students try out the author's suggestions for walking. Have them keep notes on their experiences and report back to the class. Ask students which suggestions in the article were most useful.

- *For English Language Learners* Draw attention to idiomatic phrases that may be difficult for language learners. Write phrases such as these on the board: *keep your weight down, lift the depression, take it easy, do a cool down, and*

make a date. Use each phrase in a sentence and explain its meaning so that students are comfortable with its use.

- Since most students are probably familiar with some form of fitness activity, have them compare and contrast walking to some other fitness activity. Supply a Venn diagram, and ask them to use it to tell how walking is similar to the other activity and how it is different. Have them use details from the article to support their statements.

- Challenge students to summarize the article for a person who wants to begin walking for fitness. Remind students that a summary includes the main points but omits the details. Invite volunteers to share their summaries of the article with the class.

Use reading skills: Make inferences. Explain to students that experienced readers make inferences about what they read. They are able to connect the text with what they know from their background experiences. By making inferences, they are able to extend their understanding of the content beyond the literal words of the text. In daily life, students make inferences about their friends, family members and the work they must do to meet their needs. For example, if someone sees a sign that says "For Sale" in front of a neighbor's house, they can infer that their neighbor is moving away. Help students recognize the inferences they make in their own lives.

Use a graphic organizer. The inference diagram can help students recognize their background knowledge and apply it to new information. It visually organizes what the student has read and what he or she knows. It should help students get more meaning from the text and can serve as a planning tool to organize their writing.

Write About It (PAGES 73–74)

Write a description. Have students read the directions on page 73 and be sure they understand that they will write a description of a fitness walk.

Prewriting   Have students fill in the idea map to help them begin their descriptive paragraphs. Have them brainstorm experiences they have had that can be the focus of their descriptions. Have students recall their own walks and describe the things they saw, felt, heard, and smelled. Encourage the use of sensory details to improve the descriptions.

Thinking Beyond Reading   Have students work with a partner or a small group to answer the questions. The intent is for students to probe more deeply and to elaborate on the topic by addressing issues that did not arise when they were first thinking about their walks. Encourage them to add ideas to their idea maps.

Write a draft.   Have students write independently. Write on the board the following opening sentence: *The things you hear, see, smell, and feel on a fitness walk are different from what you might experience when you walk from your car to your apartment.* Be sure students understand that all the sentences in the paragraph must relate to the same main idea, in this case the experience of a fitness walk. Remind students to use the ideas in their idea maps to organize the different elements of their responses. These will be the details in their paragraphs. Encourage them to write their thoughts quickly and freely.

Revise and create a final draft.   Remind students to use the Revising and Editing Checklist (Master 11) to guide them in revising their writing. Have students review each other's writing and give feedback on the parts of the paragraph that are logical, clear, and interesting, and the parts that need revision.

When students have finished revising their writing, use the Writing Rubric (Master 10) to evaluate it. Be sure you review your response with each student so he or she understands the strengths and weaknesses of this piece of writing. Have students date the writing and put the completed pieces in their writing portfolios.

Building Fluency

Identify small sections from "Walk On." Tell students that they will use paired reading to read these sections aloud. Put students into groups of two. Give them time to read a passage silently 2–3 times to encourage their best oral reading. Partners take turns being the reader or listener. After the first reading, the listener does not provide feedback. After the second and third readings, the listener provides feedback to the reader. Remind students to pay attention to words that cause them to stumble and to read for the author's message. Their goal is to read the passage as fluently as if they were just speaking.

Owning a Home, Losing a Home

Lesson Overview: (PAGE 75)

Theme

Have students read the lesson title on page 75 and tell them that the title introduces the lesson theme, Housing and Transportation. Discuss the theme by inviting students to share their living arrangements, telling whether they live with other family members, roommates, or alone. Ask them to mention whether they live in a house, an apartment, condo, or other housing situation.

Learning Objectives

Be sure students understand the outcome of each of the learning goals.

- *Read a story about Joyce's problems and her mortgage payments.* Point out that the story is fiction, but it describes a very real and scary problem, losing a home after a health crisis.
- *Make judgments about the decisions made by the main character.*
- *Master the key vocabulary used in the story.*
- *Write a letter to the editor.*

Preteach the vocabulary. (PAGE 75)

Read the key vocabulary words and their definitions to students. Tell them that they will recognize all these words in the story.

- Distribute the Vocabulary Knowledge Rating Chart (Master 9) and have students individually rate each of the key vocabulary words.
- Preview particularly challenging words with students by listing each one on the board, modeling its use in a sentence, and having two or three students use the word in original sentences. Reframe student sentences that do not use the new words correctly.

You may wish to offer a mini-lesson on adjectives as students read the respective parts of speech with the definitions of the vocabulary words. [See page 41 of this book for a mini-lesson on adjectives. Use Master 5 or 6 to give students practice in recognizing adjectives.]

Before You Read (PAGE 76)

Explain that good readers know when they don't understand something, and they take steps to increase understanding. Point out that good readers focus on the reading, putting question marks in the margin where they find things they do not understand. After marking a confusing passage, a good reader forms questions and then rereads to find the answers. Explain that context clues and a dictionary can help with confusing words. Rereading will also help with confusion about an element in the story's plot.

As students begin to write answers to the questions for each element on page 76, have them read aloud the respective Think About Its.

Set a purpose for reading. Use the Think About It to show that one purpose for reading is to find out how to avoid problems with buying a house. Point out that other readers may have different purposes, such as to find out how Joyce's children handled losing the house. Ask students to describe their own thinking as they set a purpose for reading the story.

Visualize while you read. Explain that good readers visualize the characters and the action in a story to help them follow what is happening. Visualizing also helps a reader remember what happened in the story. Have students read the first paragraph of the story. Then use the Think About It to demonstrate how someone might visualize the action. Invite volunteers to tell the part of the first paragraph that creates the most vivid picture in their own minds.

Reading the Story (PAGES 77–79)

Emphasize to students that they will read what happens when a homeowner has problems paying her home loan. This is a question to think about as they read. To keep them involved in the story, suggest that students highlight or mark clues to the problems Joyce has with her house.

Side-Column Vocabulary Remind students that the vocabulary words and phrases in the side column have been selected as important to the theme and content of the story. These words may be useful in the context of housing, but they are not necessarily part of everyday language.

Mid-Passage Questions Some of the answers to the questions call on students' judgments, so there are not many right or wrong answers. Review students' written answers to assess whether they are getting meaning from the text. They should indicate in their answers that Joyce lost her job as a result of her accident, which led to foreclosure. Ask students to share their feelings about Joyce's situation as well as their judgment about whether Joyce should have moved back in with her parents. Finally, ask them to speculate about whether Joyce will be able to start over. Some students may understand that defaulting on a mortgage may make it more difficult to get another mortgage.

After You Read (PAGES 80–82)

Build a robust vocabulary. Ask students to check their answers in the answer keys in their books.

Think about your reading. Ask students to check their answers in the answer keys in their books. Ask additional questions to enrich the discussion so that students will be better able to write about their own housing situations. Here are some possible questions:

- A good reader reads "between the lines." Ask students to tell what the man from the bank means when he says "You should have come and talked to us." Have them tell whether they think the bank treated Joyce fairly. Have them identify details from the story to support their answers.

- Ask students to explain why they think Joyce did not take Maria's advice. Challenge them to draw from their own experience to form a judgment.

Extend the reading. Here are some additional activities to expand students' understanding.

- At home, have students read the newspaper for a bank or mortgage service advertisement. Have them use their understanding of housing from this lesson to decipher the meaning of the advertisement. Have students bring in the ads to share with the class. Point out the elements of the ad that are mentioned in the story, "Losing a Home."

- *For English Language Learners* Since this story is told in the third person, it is a good chance for a review of pronouns and their use. Explain how a pronoun replaces a noun in English and that pronouns must match their antecedents in gender and number, for example, *she* can replace *Joyce,* but not *the two brothers.* Have students choose a paragraph from the story and mark all the pronouns. Have them identify the antecedent for each pronoun. Help students to retell the story in their own words using pronouns correctly.

- Point out to students that this story is a string of causes and effects. However, some of the earliest causes are told in the middle of the story. Have students organize the events of the story chronologically, beginning with the earliest event, when Joyce saved money to buy a house, and ending with her moving in with her parents. To help them get started, point out transition words that indicate a time order of events.

Use reading skills: Make judgments. Explain to students that a judgment is a personal decision based on their own experience and their comfort level with taking risks. Some students may say that we do dangerous things every day and that we can't avoid taking some chances. Others would say that a mother without insurance should make every effort not to endanger herself. Explain that we all make judgments about danger every day when we cross streets, drive cars, or perform our jobs. Elicit understanding that we use past experience and our own levels of confidence to make judgments in such situations. Discuss with students whether we tend to judge ourselves more harshly than we judge others.

Use a graphic organizer.   The judgment chart visually organizes the moments in the story when Joyce makes decisions. It also allows space for students to react directly. It breaks the problem into smaller, manageable parts.

Write About It (PAGES 83–84)

Write a letter to the editor.   Have students read the directions on page 83. Be sure they understand that they will write a letter to the editor in Maria's voice that explains how to avoid foreclosure.

Prewriting   Remind students that a letter to the editor can contain opinions and should be short and to the point. Have them use the graphic organizer to begin thinking about the letter, looking at the advice Maria gave Joyce to find important points. This will help them write their paragraphs in an organized manner so that their sentences logically follow each other. Encourage students to think and make notes about steering clear of foreclosure, including information from their own experiences that might be helpful.

Thinking Beyond Reading   Have students work with a partner or a small group to discuss the questions. The intent is for students to probe more deeply and to elaborate on the topic by addressing issues that did not arise when they were first thinking about how Maria would address the issue of foreclosure. Encourage them to add ideas to their webs.

Write a draft.   Have students write independently. Write on the board the following opening sentences: *My friend*

just went through the terrible experience of losing her home to foreclosure. It didn't have to happen. Here's what you can do to make sure it never happens to you. Be sure that students understand that all the sentences in the letter must relate to the same main idea, in this case how to avoid foreclosure. Remind students to use the ideas in their webs to organize the different elements of their responses. These will be the details in their paragraphs. Encourage them to write their thoughts quickly and freely.

Revise and create a final draft.   Remind students to use the Revising and Editing Checklist (Master 11) to guide them in making revisions to their writing. Have students review each other's writing and give each other feedback on the parts of the letter that are logical, clear, and interesting, and the parts that need revision.

When students have finished revising their writing, use the Writing Rubric (Master 10) to evaluate it. Be sure you review your response with each student so he or she understands the strengths and weaknesses of this piece of writing. Have students date the writing and put the completed pieces in their writing portfolios.

Building Fluency

Identify small sections from "Losing a Home." Tell students that they will use paired reading to read these sections aloud. Put students into groups of two. Give them time to read a passage silently 2–3 times to encourage their best oral reading. Partners take turns being the reader or listener. After the first reading, the listener does not provide feedback. After the second and third readings, the listener provides feedback to the reader. Remind students to pay attention to words that cause them to stumble and to read for the author's message. Their goal is to read the passage as fluently as if they were just speaking.

Healthy Eating

Lesson Overview: (PAGE 85)

Theme

Have students read the lesson title on page 85 and tell them that the title introduces the lesson theme, Food. Discuss the theme by having students make personal connections, telling about their diets and eating habits. Have them share their experience with dieting when they may have focused on healthful foods or lowering their fat intake.

Learning Objectives

Be sure students understand the outcome of each of the learning goals.

- *Learn about the fats in food.* Provide background about the article by explaining that it is nonfiction and contains detailed information about different types of fat. Explain that the vocabulary, comprehension, and writing exercises in this lesson are all related to fats in foods.
- *Learn to classify information.*
- *Master the key vocabulary used in the article.*
- *Write a description of how to lower the fat in a high-fat meal.*

Preteach the vocabulary. (PAGE 85)

Read the key vocabulary words and their definitions to the students. Tell them that they will recognize all these words in the article.

- Distribute the Vocabulary Knowledge Rating Chart (Master 9) and have students individually rate each of the key vocabulary words.
- Preview particularly challenging words with students by listing each one on the board, modeling its use in a sentence, and having two or three students use the word in original sentences. Reframe student sentences that do not use the new words correctly.

You may wish to offer a mini-lesson on nouns as students read the respective parts of speech with the definitions of the vocabulary words. [See page 39 of this book for a mini-lesson on nouns. Use Master 1 or 2 to give students practice in recognizing nouns.]

Before You Read (PAGE 86)

Explain to students that active readers do more than underline or highlight passages as they read. Suggest that they mark funny parts with *LOL* (Laughing Out Loud) or a sad face when something disappoints them. Suggest that they consider marking a Z in the margin of an article where they zone out. These notes will encourage them to pay attention to the content of the reading. Explain that the areas marked with a Z should be reviewed again. Students should try to understand what made them zone out, such as confusing vocabulary or difficult concepts.

As students begin to write answers to the questions for each element on page 86, have them read the respective Think About Its.

Use what you know. Use the Think About It to elicit a discussion about what students already know about fat. You may wish to begin a list on the board of the many kinds of fat available at the grocery store. Students may recognize that meat fat is different from vegetable oils, butter, or the fats in eggs and prepared foods, such as cookies or piecrusts.

Reread what you don't understand. Use the Think About It to help students understand when rereading is most useful. Since many sections of the article contain technical information about different types of fat, students may benefit from rereading often. Suggest that reading aloud or listening to the article being read may also help with comprehension.

Reading the Article (PAGES 87–89)

Emphasize to students that they will read about fats in the diet. Have them highlight the various types of fat they read about in the article to help keep them involved as they read.

Side-Column Vocabulary Remind students that the vocabulary words and phrases in the side column have been selected as important to the theme and content of the article. These words may be useful in the context of food, but they are not necessarily part of everyday language.

Mid-Passage Questions Review students' written answers to assess whether they are getting meaning from the text. They should indicate in their answers that people need fat in their diets for energy. Fatty acids are the building blocks of fat. Students should understand that fats should make up no more than 30% of the calories we eat, and that food labels indicate the amount of fat in many foods. Finally, students should recognize the strategies for reducing fat in the diet.

After You Read (PAGES 90–92)

Build a robust vocabulary. Ask students to check their answers in the answer keys in their books.

Think about your reading. Ask students to check their answers in the answer keys in their books. Ask additional questions to enrich the discussion so that students will be better able to write about reducing fats in the diet. Here are some possible questions:

* A good reader reads "between the lines." The author says that people need fats in their diets, but that some kinds of fat cause health problems. Does that mean that fats are good or bad? Challenge students to weigh the facts presented in the article and make judgments about how to make informed choices about fats.

* Remind students that the author says that a pat of butter has the same number of calories as an apple. Discuss this surprising fact, pointing out that an apple is much larger than a pat of butter, and that it is easy to eat too much butter at a meal.

Ask students to tell whether the fact makes them change their minds about how they should eat.

Extend the reading. Here are some additional activities to expand students' understanding.

* At home, have students collect food labels from processed foods. Have them read the information, looking for the vocabulary words from this lesson. Point out that even though food labels have many confusing words, knowing some vocabulary words having to do with fat will make some labels more familiar. Finally, discuss which foods have the fats that are suspected of causing health problems.

* *For English Language Learners* In addition to the vocabulary words, English learners may have difficulty with other technical and health-related words, such as *fatty acids, liver, heart disease, arteries, heart attack, stroke,* and *calories.* List these words on the board and offer definitions. Challenge students to find the words in the article.

* Using information in the article, have students compare and contrast the three types of fats. Have them categorize foods that contain harmful fats and fats that are less harmful. Have them include details from the text to support their comparisons.

* To help students internalize the message of the article, have them plan a day's menu with no more than 30% of its calories from fat. Discuss whether the menu is very different from students' regular diets and whether students feel the author has been persuasive in arguing that people should eat fewer fats.

Use reading skills: Classify information. Point out that different types of fat have different qualities and that remembering their differences can be confusing. Experienced readers know that sometimes they have to organize information clearly for themselves in order to understand an article completely. Classifying is how we organize confusing information into different categories. Point out that we classify information every day when we listen, read, or think. For example, when planning a shopping trip to the supermarket, we make lists by classifying what we need to buy: fresh fruit, fresh vegetables, meat, canned goods, dairy products, and so on. Ask students to offer other examples of ways that they classify information in their daily living.

Use a graphic organizer.   The classifying chart can help students analyze the information from the article. It can also serve as a planning tool to organize their thinking. In this case, the chart allows students to recognize the different kinds of fats.

Write About It (PAGES 93–94)

Write a description.   Have students read the directions on page 93. Be sure they understand that they will write a descriptive paragraph about how they could lower the fat content in a meal they have made.

Prewriting   Remind students to use the chart to begin thinking about how ingredients and cooking methods can help lower the kinds and amounts of fat in meals. This chart will help them write their descriptions so that their sentences logically follow each other. Encourage students to describe how to lower the high fat content in their meals by using ingredients and cooking methods that don't sacrifice great taste.

Thinking Beyond Reading   Have students work with a partner or a small group to discuss the questions. The intent is for students to think more clearly about the fat in their meals and to find ways to make the meals lower in fat. Encourage students to add ideas to their classifying charts.

Write a draft.   Have students write independently. Write on the board the following possible opening sentences:

My family often eats a high-fat meal of steak, mashed potatoes, green beans with butter, and ice cream. But there are ways to reduce fat in our meal without losing any of the flavor. Clarify that the opening sentences should name the foods they have chosen for their meals. Be sure that students understand that all the sentences in the paragraph must relate to the same main idea, in this case a description of a delicious, high-fat meal that can still be delicious without all that fat. Remind students to use the notes from their classifying charts as they write. Encourage them to write their thoughts quickly and freely.

Revise and create a final draft.   Remind students to use the Revising and Editing Checklist (Master 11) to guide them in revising their writing. Have students review each other's writing and give feedback on the parts of the paragraph that are logical, clear, and interesting, and the parts that need revision.

When students have finished revising their writing, use the Writing Rubric (Master 10) to evaluate it. Be sure you review your response with each student so he or she understands the strengths and weaknesses of this piece of writing. Have students date the writing and put the completed pieces in their writing portfolios.

Building Fluency

Identify small sections from "Know Your Fats." Tell students that they will use echo reading to read these sections aloud. Put students into groups of two. Give them time to read a passage silently 2–3 times to encourage their best oral reading. Remind them to pay attention to words that cause them to stumble. They will imitate your phrasing and intonation for each sentence. Remind students to use punctuation and typographic cues to add expression to their reading. Tell them that the goal is to read the passage as fluently as if they were just speaking.

Being Money Smart

Lesson Overview: (PAGE 95)

Theme

Have students read the lesson title on page 95 and tell them that the title introduces the lesson theme, Consumerism and Money. Discuss the theme by having students make personal connections, telling how they keep track of their paychecks each week.

Learning Objectives

Be sure the students understand the outcome of each of the learning goals.

- *Learn about payday loans.* Offer background by explaining that the article is nonfiction and that the author has an opinion about the topic.
- *Determine if a statement is a fact or an opinion.*
- *Master the key vocabulary used in the article.*
- *Write an e-mail to a friend that warns about the dangers of payday loans.*

Preteach the vocabulary. (PAGE 95)

Read the key vocabulary words and their definitions to students. Tell them that they will recognize all these words in the article.

- Distribute the Vocabulary Knowledge Rating Chart (Master 9) and have students individually rate each of the key vocabulary words.
- Preview particularly challenging words with students by listing each one on the board, modeling its use in a sentence, and having two or three students use the word in original sentences. Reframe student sentences that do not use the new words correctly.

You may wish to offer a mini-lesson on nouns as students read the respective parts of speech with the definitions of the vocabulary words. [See page 39 of this book for a mini-lesson on nouns. Use Master 1 or 2 to give students practice in recognizing nouns.]

Before You Read (PAGE 96)

Point out that active readers ask questions as they read. Questions could be things that the reader wants to learn from the text or things that the reader cannot understand. Explain to students the four strategies for finding answers to questions: First, reread the text and try to understand confusing passages. Second, stop and think about what you already know from your own experience and what you can conclude about the new information. Third, use a reference book such as a dictionary to look up difficult words. Finally, if all else fails, ask for help from a teacher or classmate. Encourage students to mark the answers to their questions in the text so that the answers are readily available when they review the lesson.

As students begin to write answers to the questions for each element on page 96, have them read aloud the respective Think About Its.

Set a purpose for reading. Use the Think About It to elicit a conversation about what students know about payday loan shops and their opinions about them. Remind students that setting a purpose for reading helps keep a reader focused on the information in the article.

Ask yourself questions. Explain that the article may contain information that is confusing or complicated. Asking questions is a good way to identify the areas where students need help. Add to the list with students' other questions.

Reading the Article (PAGES 97–99)

Emphasize to students that they are reading to find out more about payday loans and why such loans may not be a good choice. Highlighting phrases that are clues to the problems with loan shops is a strategy that will keep them involved in the article.

Side-Column Vocabulary Remind students that the vocabulary words and phrases in the side column have been selected as important to the theme and content of the article. These words may be useful in the context of money and loans, but they are not necessarily part of everyday language.

Mid-Passage Questions   Some of the answers call for students' opinions, so there are not many right or wrong answers. Review students' written answers to assess whether they are getting meaning from the text. They should indicate in their answers that June probably does not understand the fees she is racking up as she rolls over her loan. They should understand that the Truth in Lending Act requires lenders to explain clearly the interest rate on a loan. Students should identify the techniques payday lenders use to lure customers, and share any personal experience they have with such loans. Finally, students should understand the suggested techniques for avoiding such loans.

After You Read (PAGES 100–102)

Build a robust vocabulary.   Ask students to check their answers in the answer keys in their books.

Think about your reading.   Ask students to check their answers in the answer keys in their books. Ask additional questions to enrich the discussion so that students will be better able to write about payday loans. Here are some possible questions.

- A good reader reads "between the lines." What did the author want you to learn from June's experiences? What can you infer about June from this sentence, "By the time she had rolled over the loan three times, she had paid $60 in interest for her $100 loan"?

- Why do payday lenders advertise for new customers with gifts and prizes? Why do you think the author feels these tactics are not appropriate? Encourage students to discuss whether payday loan lenders offer a service or prey on the poor.

Extend the Reading   Here are some additional activities to expand students' understanding.

- At home, have students gather offers that come from their banks about overdraft protection or

loans or other banking arrangements. Encourage them to read the paragraphs carefully, circling words they do not understand. Look for details about interest rates and the terms of banking agreements. Have students share what they learned with the class by bringing the offers to share with classmates.

- *For English Language Learners*   Since the banking system in the U.S. may be different from their own past experiences, ask English learners to make a comparison between the banking system in their homeland and that in the U.S. Set up a chart with words, such as *credit rating, checking account, overdraft* and so on, and have English learners fill in the chart with the corresponding words from their own languages.

- Point out to students that the author uses loaded words to help persuade the reader. Write the following words on the board: *pounce, desperate, greedy, lure, thriving, predatory, bright spot,* and *in a pinch.* Discuss how certain words have connotations that are negative or positive. The author uses loaded words to impose a judgment about a topic. Have students work in pairs to make lists of other loaded words and then have them share their lists with the class. Help them get started by asking if *specialty coffee* is a positive or a negative phrase. Students may be interested in using what they have learned about loaded words to rewrite a part of the article from the perspective of a payday lender.

Use reading skills: Identify fact and opinion.   Begin by explaining the differences between facts and opinions. Then follow the discussion by explaining why it matters whether a reader can tell the difference. Tell students that just because a person believes something, that does not make it true. Good readers use the facts in an article and form their own opinions. This strategy is useful in real life too. For example, a payday loan store may make it seem like such a loan is a great idea. However, sorting fact from opinion will help students find the truth. Ask them to share their own experience with being swayed by someone else's opinion. Ask them to share how they might have handled the situation differently.

Use a graphic organizer. The fact and opinion chart helps separate information into those details that can be proven and those that are based on one person's beliefs. The chart will help students understand when the author is stating his or her own ideas.

Write About It (PAGES 103–104)

Write an e-mail. Have students read the directions on page 103 and be sure they understand that they will write an e-mail stating their opinion about a proposed law about payday loans.

Prewriting Remind students how to use the idea web as they collect their ideas for the e-mail. Point out that they should begin with an opinion statement and back it up with details from the article and from their own experience.

Thinking Beyond Reading Have students work with a partner or a small group to discuss the questions. The intent is for students to probe more deeply and to elaborate on the topic by addressing issues that did not arise when they were first thinking about the e-mail. Encourage them to add ideas to their idea webs.

Write a draft. Have students write independently. Be sure they understand that all the sentences in the e-mail must relate to the opinion statement about payday loans. Remind students to use the points in their idea webs to organize their writing. Web details should be mentioned in the e-mail. Encourage students to write their thoughts quickly and freely.

Revise and create a final draft. Remind students to use the Revising and Editing Checklist (Master 11) to guide them in making revisions to their writing. Have students review each other's writing and give feedback on the parts of the e-mail that are logical, clear, and interesting, and the parts that need revision.

When students have finished revising their writing, use the Writing Rubric (Master 10) to evaluate it. Be sure you review your response with each student so he or she understands the strengths and weaknesses of this piece of writing. Have students date the writing and put the completed pieces in their writing portfolios.

Building Fluency

Identify small sections from "Payday Loans: Beware!" Tell students that they will use paired reading to read these sections aloud. Put students into groups of two. Give them time to read a passage silently 2–3 times to encourage their best oral reading. Partners take turns being the reader or listener. After the first reading, the listener does not provide feedback. After the second and third readings, the listener provides feedback to the reader. Remind students to pay attention to words that cause them to stumble and to read for the author's message. Their goal is to read the passage as fluently as if they were just speaking.

Grammar Mini-Lessons

LESSON 1: NOUNS

Learning Objectives

To define the term *noun*

To identify nouns

To generate nouns

Activate Prior Knowledge

Help students realize what they already know about *nouns.* Ask a volunteer to name a job title, for example, *nurse.* Then ask another volunteer where someone doing that job works *(a hospital).* Have the next volunteer name something that person uses on the job *(bandages),* and finally have a volunteer name a quality required in that job *(kindness).* Point out that all these words are **nouns.**

Instruction

Tell the class that **nouns are the names of people, places, things, and ideas.** Write this definition on the board. Tell them they are going to help you create a noun chart.

Examples of Nouns			
People	**Places**	**Things**	**Ideas**

Ask: *What names of people, places, things, and ideas do you come across every day?* Have students take turns giving examples. Write them on the board in the appropriate columns. Encourage the class to help you fill in the chart.

If students suggest proper nouns, include them. Point out to students that proper nouns can be more than one word (a person's name, for example). Also point out that proper nouns are written with a capital letter at the beginning of each word.

If students need more examples, write each underlined word in the appropriate column of the chart as you say the following aloud: *When you are traveling, do you see <u>cabbies</u> driving their <u>taxis</u> on the <u>street</u>? And what <u>quality</u> might a <u>passenger</u> want in a <u>cabbie</u>? They probably want <u>speed</u>, <u>safety</u>, and <u>courtesy</u>.* You can do similar exercises describing a bank teller or a doctor.

If students seem to be having difficulty with "ideas" as nouns, consider telling them the following: *The names of ideas are not things that you can touch with your hands. But they are still nouns, just like names of people, places, and things.* Examples might include the names of emotions, such as *happiness* or *sadness, excitement* or *boredom.* Other ideas include conditions, such as *poverty* or *wealth, safety* or *danger.*

Noun Practice

For more student practice with nouns, distribute Master 1 or 2 in this Teacher's Guide.

LESSON 2: VERBS

Learning Objectives
To define the term *verb*

To identify verbs

To generate verbs

Activate Prior Knowledge
Help students recall or discover what they already know about *verbs*. Ask the class if they ever played "Simon Says" when they were children or with their own children. If not, have a volunteer explain the rules. (A leader tells a group to do things. The group should only obey when the leader first says "Simon says." Those who do not follow this rule are out.)

Now, play "Simon Says." As quickly as you can, call out instructions. (Examples: *Simon says lift your arms. Simon says smile. Clap your hands.*)

Tell students that you were asking them to perform actions and that the words you used (*lift, smile, clap*) are **verbs,** words that show action.

Instruction
Write the word *run* on the board. Direct the class to think of words that mean *to run*. Then ask volunteers to say their words. (Examples: *dash, sprint, race, hurtle, dart, rush, scurry, bolt, fly, speed*) Tell the class that these words are *verbs*. Write on the board: **Words that show action are called verbs.**

Then write the following three words on the board: *yawns, red, cat.* Ask students to name the word or words that show action *(yawns)*.

Write on the board three columns of three words. In each column include at least one verb. Have volunteers underline the verbs. Warn them that there might be one, two, or even three verbs in a group. Examples:

<u>opens</u>	town	<u>invites</u>
Joey	crackers	<u>spills</u>
<u>chews</u>	<u>jumps</u>	<u>follows</u>

paper	middle	earth
<u>cures</u>	<u>enjoys</u>	<u>turns</u>
round	<u>laughs</u>	globe

Finally, write a sentence on the board, leaving spaces for two verbs. (Example: *The cat _____ and _____ all day long.*) Have volunteers orally fill in the blanks with verbs. (Examples: *purrs/sleeps, eats/scratches, plays/jumps.*)

Encourage students to compose oral sentences that use two verbs. Model the sentences for them by writing on the board: *All day yesterday I _____ and _____. All day tomorrow I will _____ and _____.* Point out that the verbs they use show past time and future time.

You may wish to point out to the class that the same word can sometimes be a verb and sometimes a noun. (Examples: *show, smile, watch, hide, drop, sock, award, knock.*) If they understand this concept, encourage students to find words that can be either verbs or nouns in newspapers or magazines at home.

Verb Practice
For more student practice with verbs, distribute Master 3 or 4 in this Teacher's Guide.

LESSON 3: ADJECTIVES

Learning Objectives

To define the term *adjective*

To identify adjectives

To generate adjectives

Activate Prior Knowledge

Help students recall or find out what they already know about *adjectives*. Ask them to name some vegetables. Encourage them to describe each type of vegetable they name. As they talk, write their adjectives on the board. (Examples: *raw, green, leafy, crisp,* and *sweet.*) Tell the class that these words are **adjectives.**

Instruction

Tell the class that **adjectives are words that describe nouns.** Then elicit from students some common nouns. Write the words *Adjectives* and *Nouns* on the board. Under *Adjectives* draw blank lines. Under *Nouns* write the common nouns the class provides. Your chart might look like this:

Adjectives	Nouns
	chair
	lake
	building

Then ask the class to think of a one-word description for each noun. (Examples: *soft* and *old, clear* and *cold, tall* and *huge.*) Call on volunteers to write their descriptive words in the blanks on the board. Then ask volunteers to create sentences using the nouns and their adjectives. (Examples: *I like the soft chair. I enjoy swimming in that clear lake. I want to live in that tall building.*)

Tell students to look for restaurant reviews in newspapers or magazines. Have each cut out a review and read it. As they read, they should underline the nouns and then circle the adjectives that describe them. Tell them that not all the nouns will have adjectives. To help them focus their efforts, give them some examples of the language they might find in their reviews, such as *excellent food, poor service, fresh fruit,* or *generous portions.*

Suggest that after reading the review, they might want to review a meal that they were served or one that they made themselves. They may do this orally or in writing. Encourage them to use some of the adjectives they found in the newspaper reviews.

Adjective Practice

For more student practice with adjectives, distribute Master 5 or 6 in this Teacher's Guide.

LESSON 4: ADVERBS

Learning Objectives
To define the term *adverb*

To identify adverbs

To generate adverbs

Activate Prior Knowledge
Help students discover what they know about *adverbs*. Whisper to a volunteer: *Walk to the front of the room in slow motion.* As the volunteer proceeds, ask the class: *What is he doing? (walking slowly)* Then ask: *How is he walking? (slowly)* Tell the class that *slowly* is an adverb. It describes the verb *walk* and tells how he is walking.

Instruction
Tell the class that **adverbs are words that describe verbs.** They tell how, when, or where. Draw the following chart on the board.

Verb	How?	When?	Where?
walk			

Point to the second column and ask the class to tell you: *How did [volunteer's name] walk? (slowly)* Point to the third column and ask: *When did he walk? (today) Where did he walk? (inside)* Tell them the words *slowly, today,* and *inside* are all adverbs. They describe the verb *walk*.

Now elicit two or three more verbs. Write them in the first column. Then for each one ask students to provide the adverbs. Encourage students by pointing to and asking the questions at the top of each column. (Example: *Run—How did he run? Quickly; When did he run? Yesterday; Where did he run? Outside.*)

You may wish to read the examples students give to you in the order in which the adverbs make the most sense. (Examples: *He walked slowly today inside. Yesterday, he ran outside quickly. I always write neatly here in class. Always go backward cautiously.*)

Point out to students that adverbs may appear anywhere in a sentence. Often they are close to the verb, but sometimes they are not. Write examples on the board. As you describe where the verb and adverb are located, underline the verb and draw an arrow from the verb to the adverb. Examples:

He <u>rushed</u> frantically to the burning car.

Frantically, he <u>rushed</u> to the car.

He <u>rushed</u> to the car frantically.

Adverb Practice
For more student practice with adverbs, distribute Master 7 or 8 in this Teacher's Guide.

Master 1: Nouns 1

Student's Name _____

A noun is the name of a person, place, thing, or idea.

Examples of nouns are listed in the chart below.

People	Places	Things	Ideas
children gardener	downown street	seeds vegetables	friendship wealth

Finding Nouns: Underline the nouns in each sentence.

1. Your skeleton is the framework of your body.

2. Vitamins and minerals make bones strong.

3. Bones need the calcium in certain foods.

4. Experts tell us to include fiber in our diets.

5. People should also drink eight cups of water each day.

6. Exercise and good nutrition contribute to good health.

Writing Nouns: Read the nouns in the box below. Write one noun in each sentence.

laughter	permission	pride	relationships	vegetables	volunteers

7. Neighbors want to grow _____ in the vacant lot.

8. The owner of the land gave them _____ to use it.

9. Many _____ showed up on the first day.

10. People can build friendly _____ when they plan the garden.

11. You can hear the sound of _____ as people talk and work.

12. Everyone felt _____ in the work that was done.

Using Nouns: Write a noun to complete each sentence.

13. My _____ eats sunflower seeds as a snack.

14. He skillfully built a _____ for the garden.

15. Go to the _____ to buy ripe peaches and plums.

Master 2: Nouns 2

Student's Name

> **A noun is the name of a person, place, thing, or idea.**

Examples of nouns are listed in the chart below. Some are common nouns. They are the general names for people, places, or things. Proper nouns are the names of specific people, places, or things.

	Common Nouns	**Proper Nouns**
People	student	Paul Winfield
Places	country	The United States
Things	airline	National Airlines

Finding Nouns: Underline the proper nouns.

1. The last grizzly bear was killed in California.

2. The golden trout swims in the Kern River near Mount Whitney.

3. Every year people in Los Angeles celebrate Labor Day.

4. The San Diego Zoo is a popular place for families to visit.

5. Early in his career Ansel Adams worked for *Time* magazine.

6. John Muir helped to protect Yosemite National Park.

Writing Nouns: Circle the common nouns. Underline and capitalize the proper nouns.

7. The first people in california may have come from asia.

8. Some tribes are named mojave and shoshone.

9. Soldiers and priests from spain settled in san diego.

10. Governor arnold schwarzenegger is a bodybuilder who was born in austria.

Using Nouns: Write proper nouns to complete the sentences.

11. The name of a street in my town is _____.

12. A store in my neighborhood is called _____.

13. I started school in the month of _____.

14. My favorite store is _____.

15. My favorite sports team is _____.

Master 3: Verbs 1

Student's Name _____

A verb is a word that shows action.

The underlined words are verbs. They show action.

Clowns <u>play</u>.	Soldiers <u>march</u>.	Tigers <u>roar</u>.
Whistles <u>blow</u>.	Worms <u>slither</u>.	Roads <u>wind</u>.

Finding Verbs: Circle the verb in each sentence.

1. Chris Rock earned many Emmy Awards.

2. He admires Sugar Ray Leonard and Eddie Murphy.

3. Chris describes everyday events with humor.

4. My son watches his television show often.

5. He tickles my imagination with his stories.

6. The audience shook the theater with laughter.

7. The comic's point of view surprises me.

Writing Verbs: Find each verb. Then write each verb on the line provided. HINT: Two sentences have more than one verb.

8. Some city people raise pigeons as pets. _____

9. The birds perch on tree branches and roof ledges. _____

10. Pigeons swallow grains, seeds, and small stones. _____

11. They waddle and coo inside their cages. _____

12. Homing pigeons soar over long distances. _____

13. Seagulls dive for fish in the waters. _____

14. Bird lovers wait and search the sky. _____

Using Verbs: Read the verbs. Then write a new verb with the opposite meaning.

Example: laugh __cry_____

15. scream _____

16. float _____

17. win _____

18. forget _____

19. give _____

20. push _____

21. arrive _____

22. throw _____

23. love _____

24. lend _____

Master 4: Verbs 2

Student's Name _____

> **A verb is a word that shows action.**

The underlined words are verbs.

Verbs	Time of Action
A batter <u>practices</u> on the field.	present
The catcher <u>sprained</u> his wrist.	past
They <u>will win</u> the game.	future

Finding Verbs: The verb in each sentence is underlined. Circle the time it shows.

1. Visitors <u>will wonder</u> at this great tribute.   future   present

2. Mayor Bloomberg <u>spoke</u> to the crowd.   present   past

3. The monument <u>celebrates</u> two great ball players.   future   present

4. Robinson <u>joined</u> the majors in the 1940s.   past   future

5. Reese <u>drapes</u> his arm around Robinson.   past   present

6. Their friendship <u>will endure</u>.   present   future

Writing Verbs: Underline the verb in each sentence. Then write the verb on the line provided.

7. People cherish the memory of Roberto Clemente. _____

8. His career inspires baseball fans of all ages. _____

9. He died on New Year's Eve in 1972. _____

10. He earned the Presidential Medal of Freedom. _____

11. We will remember him as a hero. _____

Using Verbs: Underline the verbs. Then write each verb to show a different time.

Example: The batter waited for his turn. __will wait_____

12. Rain pours on the empty stadium. _____

13. The last inning thrilled the fans. _____

14. The crowd roars with excitement. _____

15. The ball explodes into the outfield. _____

16. The player climbed the fence. _____

Master 5: Adjectives 1

Student's Name

> **An adjective is a word that describes a noun.**

The adjectives in the sentences below are underlined.

> <u>Three</u> people are in the kitchen.
> The air is filled with <u>spicy</u> smells.
> I love <u>black</u> beans and rice.

Finding Adjectives: The first column is a list of nouns. Draw a line to connect each noun to an adjective. The first one is done for you.

ADJECTIVES	NOUNS
1. hungry	• seed
2. heavy	• shovel
3. tiny	• birds
4. cool	• leaves
5. green	• shade

Writing Adjectives: Read the sentences. Each noun is underlined. Write the adjective that describes the noun.

6. She looked down from the tall <u>building</u>. _____

7. Several <u>children</u> played ball on the street. _____

8. A broken <u>broom</u> was the bat. _____

9. The ball rolled under a small <u>truck</u>. _____

10. A boy with long <u>arms</u> found it. _____

Using Adjectives: Write an adjective to describe each noun.

11. _____ radio

12. _____ automobiles

13. _____ garage

14. _____ skyscraper

15. _____ buses

Master 6: Adjectives 2

Student's Name _____

An adjective is a word that describes a noun.

The adjectives in the sentences below are underlined.

Two girls picked red tomatoes.
Their new hats had wide brims.
The happy children ate a big lunch.

Finding Adjectives: Circle the adjectives.

1. Eleven men started new jobs last week.

2. One man wore the same shirt and pants every day.

3. Another man wore clean clothes.

4. His careful appearance showed he cared.

5. He used his first paycheck to buy new clothes.

6. The young manager noticed the proud man.

Writing Adjectives: Read the adjectives in the box below. Then write one on each line.

young	big	fat	pretty	black	old	little	skinny	ugly	white

7. The _____ dog wagged his _____ tail.

8. The _____ kitten meowed in its _____ cage.

9. The _____ salesman talked to the _____ shopper.

10. The _____ woman chose her pet.

11. The _____ animal slept on the blanket.

Using Adjectives: Write an adjective to complete each sentence.

12. She got out of her _____ bed.

13. She put on her _____ dress.

14. She ate a bowl of _____ cereal.

15. She drank a _____ cup of coffee.

16. She washed the _____ dishes.

Master 7: Adverbs 1

Student's Name _____

> **An adverb is a word that describes a verb.**

These words are adverbs. They tell how, when, and where.

How?	quickly, sadly, carefully, boldly
When?	sometimes, yesterday, never, often
Where?	inside, here, forward, nowhere

Finding Adverbs: Read the sentences. Verbs are underlined. Circle the adverbs that describe them.

1. Muhammad Ali <u>lives</u> here in the United States.

2. He firmly <u>believes</u> in doing his best at all times.

3. He <u>fought</u> tirelessly for freedom and justice.

4. He always <u>loved</u> words as a kind of entertainment.

5. His wit <u>changed</u> forever the image of a champion.

6. Proudly, he <u>called</u> himself the greatest and proved he was.

Writing Adverbs: Find the adverb in each sentence. Write it on the line.

7. Roman slaves fought gladly for their freedom. _____

8. Free men boxed there, too. _____

9. Wisely, the English made up rules for safety. _____

10. A referee watches the fighters closely. _____

11. Fans follow the winners everywhere. _____

12. Today, people see fights on television. _____

Using Adverbs: Read the adverbs in the box below. Choose an adverb to complete each sentence.

again	here	often	outside	nearby	now	soon	today

13. You can wrestle _____.

14. You can ski _____.

15. You can sprint _____.

16. You can race _____.

17. You can tumble _____.

18. You can swim _____.

19. You can skate _____.

20. You can jump _____.

Master 8: Adverbs 2

Student's Name _____

| **An adverb is a word that describes a verb.** |

Adverbs are the underlined words in the sentences below. They describe verbs by telling how, when, and where. Arrows point to the verbs.

She eagerly listens to his show. (listens how?)

He reported the story today. (reported when?)

The heavy rains fell everywhere. (fell where?)

Finding Adverbs: The verbs are underlined. Circle each adverb that describes a verb.

1. Hurricanes hit that area often.

2. Unfortunately, the storm destroyed much of the coast.

3. The levee system failed the city completely.

4. The brave rescuer searched inside.

5. The rain and wind pushed him backward.

6. Finally, he found the ones who survived.

7. The family waited impatiently.

8. They expect the helicopter now.

9. It landed there on the rooftop.

Writing Adverbs: Write the adverbs you circled in the correct column.

How?	When?	Where?
10.	13.	16.
11.	14.	17.
12.	15.	18.

Using Adverbs: Choose an adverb from the list to complete each sentence.

| happily | fearfully | carefully | quickly | softly |

19. She watched the storm _____.

20. She whispered _____ to him.

21. She _____ lifted the broken glass.

22. She ran across the street _____.

23. She found a new home _____.

Master 9: Vocabulary Knowledge Rating Chart Student's Name

1	2	3	4	5
Vocabulary Word	I know this word. I can explain its meaning and use it when I speak and write.	I think I know this word. It has something to do with _____.	I've seen or heard this word, but I'm not sure what it means.	I don't know this word. I need to learn it.

Master 10: Writing Rubric

Student's Name

	Focus	Organization	Voice	Conventions
4	Ideas are on the topic and interesting.	There is a clearly presented main idea with supporting details, facts, and/or opinions. The writing flows very well.	The writer speaks to the audience clearly. Word choice is varied, and the words were chosen because they are the very best words for getting the point across.	Contains few, if any, errors in grammar, punctuation, capitalization, and/or spelling. Any errors that do occur do not get in the way of the reader's understanding.
3	Ideas are on the topic.	There is a main idea with supporting details, facts, and/or opinions. The writing flows.	The writer speaks to the audience. Word choice is varied and gets the point across.	Contains some errors in grammar, punctuation, capitalization, and/or spelling. These errors do not get in the way of the reader's understanding.
2	Ideas may be a bit off of the topic.	Although there is a main idea and/or details, the writing is sometimes difficult to follow.	The writer shows some understanding of the audience. Words are repeated too often and/or misused.	Contains several errors in grammar, punctuation, capitalization, and/or spelling. These errors may get in the way of the reader's understanding of the writing.
1	Ideas are not on the topic.	It is difficult for the reader to follow the writer's arguments or explanations.	The writer does not speak to the audience. Words are repeated too often and/or misused.	Contains serious errors in grammar, punctuation, capitalization, and/or spelling. These errors make the writing very difficult for the reader to understand.

Master 11: Revising and Editing Checklist   Student's Name

When you **revise,** you add to or take away from your writing to make it clearer and more understandable. It always helps to read your work to a partner so that you can make sure it is well organized, includes enough details, and makes sense.

When you **edit,** look at the specific words you have chosen. Are they the best words? Check your work for proper spelling, punctuation, and usage. Make sure that you have not left out or repeated words. Have you used correct grammar?

Always revise before you edit. You don't want to spend time editing something you may not include in your revision.

Revising

_____ I read the writing to myself to see if it made sense.

_____ I read the writing to a partner to see if it made sense.

_____ My writing stays on the topic.

_____ My paragraph has a topic sentence and includes supporting details.

_____ My writing is logical and well organized.

_____ The writing is interesting.

_____ I used enough information and examples to make my point.

_____ My ending ties up the writing.

Editing

_____ Each of my sentences ends with a period (.), a question mark (?), or an exclamation point (!).

_____ My subjects and verbs agree.

_____ I have used commas correctly.

_____ Each of my sentences begins with a capital letter.

_____ I have used quotation marks correctly.

_____ My paragraphs are indented.

_____ I chose my words carefully so that the reader can visualize just what I'm talking about.

_____ I inserted words that add interest to my writing.

_____ I inserted words that were missing.

_____ I deleted extra words that I didn't need.

_____ I circled words that I think may be incorrectly spelled. I used additional resources to check the spelling of those words.

_____ I gave my edited draft to a partner to check.

Master 12: Editor's Marks

Student's Name

Use these marks when editing a paper. Make sure you understand what the marks mean when a teacher or partner uses them on your paper.

Editing Marks		
☰	Changes a lowercase letter to an uppercase letter.	I visited kiwanis park with my cousins.
/	Changes an uppercase letter to a lowercase letter.	Maria brought her Dog.
∧	Adds a word or punctuation mark.	We biked the park. (to)
ℓ	Deletes a word or punctuation mark.	We ran around the the playground.
☐	Indicates incorrect word choice.	We had a lot of fun their (there)
◯	Indicates a misspelled word.	We plan to go agin next weekend. (again)

Answers to Masters 1–8

MASTER 1: NOUNS 1

1. skeleton, framework, body
2. Vitamins, minerals, bones
3. Bones, calcium, foods
4. Experts, fiber, diets
5. People, cups, water, day
6. Exercise, nutrition, health
7. vegetables
8. permission
9. volunteers
10. relationships
11. laughter
12. pride
13.–15. Answers will vary

MASTER 2: NOUNS 2

1. California
2. Kern River, Mount Whitney
3. Los Angeles, Labor Day
4. San Diego Zoo
5. Ansel Adams, *Time* magazine
6. John Muir, Yosemite National Park
7. people, California, Asia
8. tribes, Mojave, Shoshone
9. Soldiers, priests, Spain, San Diego
10. bodybuilder, Governor Arnold Schwarzenegger, Austria
11.–15. Answers will vary

MASTER 3: VERBS 1

1. earned
2. admires
3. describes
4. watches
5. tickles
6. shook
7. surprises
8. raise
9. perch
10. swallow
11. waddle, coo
12. soar
13. dive
14. wait, search
15. whisper
16. sink
17. lose
18. remember
19. take
20. pull
21. leave
22. catch
23. hate
24. borrow

MASTER 4: VERBS 2

1. future
2. past
3. present
4. past
5. present
6. future
7. cherish
8. inspires
9. died
10. earned
11. will remember
12. poured, *or* will pour
13. thrills, *or* will thrill
14. roared, *or* will roar
15. exploded, *or* will explode
16. climbs, *or* will climb

MASTER 5: ADJECTIVES 1

2. heavy shovel
3. tiny seed
4. cool shade
5. green leaves
6. tall
7. Several
8. broken
9. small
10. long
11.–15. Answers will vary

MASTER 6: ADJECTIVES 2

1. Eleven, new, last
2. One, same, every
3. Another, clean
4. careful
5. first, new
6. young, proud
7.–16. Answers will vary.

MASTER 7: ADVERBS 1

1. here
2. firmly
3. tirelessly
4. always
5. forever
6. Proudly
7. gladly
8. there
9. Wisely
10. closely
11. everywhere
12. Today
13.–20. Answers will vary

MASTER 8: ADVERBS 2

1. often
2. Unfortunately
3. completely
4. inside
5. backward
6. Finally
7. impatiently
8. now
9. there
10. Unfortunately
11. completely
12. impatiently
13. often
14. Finally
15. now
16. inside
17. backward
18. there
19.–23. Answers will vary.
Possible answers:
19. fearfully
20. softly
21. carefully
22. quickly
23. happily